CHARLIE TROTTER'S

A day of fine cooking begins with firing up the line.

Also in the Great Restaurants of the World series:

Café des Artistes
Commander's Palace
The Inn at Little Washington
The Sardine Factory

CHARLIE TROTTER'S

An Insider's Look at the Famed Restaurant and Its Cuisine

Edmund Lawler

Photographs by Michael Voltattorni

Lebhar-Friedman Books

New York • Chicago • Los Angeles • London • Paris • Tokyo

Lebhar-Friedman Books
425 Park Avenue
New York, NY 10022

Published by Lebhar-Friedman Books
Lebhar-Friedman Books is a company of Lebhar-Friedman, Inc.

Great Restaurants of the World® is a trademark
of Lebhar-Friedman Books.

Printed in the United States of America

Library of Congress Cataloging-in-Publication Data

Lawler, Edmund O.
    Charlie Trotter's : an insider's look at the famed restaurant
and its cuisine / Edmund O. Lawler.

    .

        p. cm. — (Great restaurants of the world)
    ISBN 0-86730-803-6 (alk. paper)
    1. Charlie Trotter's (Restaurant). 2. Trotter, Charlie.
3. Cookery. I. Title. II. Series.

    TX945.5.C365 L39 2000
    641.5'09773'11—dc21

                                    99-059970

Book design: Nancy Koch, NK Design

An SCI production

Jacket design: Kevin Hanek
Photographs © 2000 by Michael Voltattorni

Visit our Web site at lfbooks.com

Dedication

To two very dear people, Ruth and Herb Stegemiller

Acknowledgments

Thanks to Charlie Trotter, his family, and his staff for their cooperation and patience. A special thanks to the restaurant's Mark Signorio for even larger measures of cooperation and patience. Thanks also to my editor, Martin Everett, for his thoughtful handling of the manuscript.

About the author

Edmund O. Lawler teaches journalism at DePaul University.

Photograph: © Tim Turner

Prior to his academic career, he was a journalist for more than 20 years. He was a writer for the Chicago bureau of the Associated Press, business editor of the *Indianapolis News,* and managing editor of *Business Marketing* magazine. He still writes the magazine's popular "Copy Chasers" column. Lawler is the author of *Copy Chasers on Creating Business-to-Business Ads* and *Underdog Marketing: Successful Strategies to Outmarket the Leader.* He is coauthor of *Marketing Masters: Secrets of America's Best Companies.*

Lawler has a degree in journalism from Drake University and a master's degree in government and international studies from the University of Notre Dame. He lives in Chicago with his wife, Priscilla, and their sons, Griff and Bryan.

About the photographer

Michael Voltattorni is a Chicago fashion photographer whose work has been featured in such publications as *Allure, Chicago, Entertainment Weekly, Chicago Social,* the *Chicago Tribune, Ocean Drive,* and *Town & Country.* He is known for his celebrity portraits and CD covers and for his work on advertising campaigns for Coca-Cola, Hubbard Street Dance Co., Bigsby & Kruthers, and Paul Stuart.

CONTENTS

FOREWORD

Few experiences in life enhance the joy of living more than a fine dining experience. The ambience, style, service, food, and presentation of a great restaurant are all elements that add immensely to enjoying a culinary adventure. Many restaurants provide customers with a consistent dining experience, and a number of these are truly outstanding. Only a few, however, exceed the expectations of even their most discerning patrons. They deserve to be called great, and we are proud to recognize them

as Great Restaurants of the World. The first five restaurants in this series of books are:

Charlie Trotter's
Café des Artistes
Commander's Palace
The Inn at Little Washington
The Sardine Factory

These beautiful books have been a labor of love and dedication for all the parties involved. We have called upon the editors of *Nation's Restaurant News,* the leading business publication serving the restaurant industry, to assist us in developing the criteria for the Great Restaurants of the World series and in choosing the candidates. We think you will agree that the selections are of great interest and merit.

All of the Great Restaurants of the World represent a unique creative spirit of providing the public with a meaningful dining experience. However, they also share many of the same traits. Most significantly, each was founded by one or more persons with the kind of entrepreneurial energy dedicated to achieving excellence. Without exception, these founders instilled in their organizations a single compelling mission: to provide their guests with the ultimate dining experience. Food and food presentation are always the first priority. After that come service, ambience, and value.

All of these restaurants have been successful by paying attention to innumerable small details every day, every week, and every month throughout the year. Each has proved many times over its reputation as a truly great restaurant through the loyalty of its repeat customers and the steady stream of awards and recognition it has received over the years, both from its guests and from its peers.

This book and the others in the series are your invitation to experience the Great Restaurants of the World, their history and their heritage. Savor every page and enjoy the adventure.

James C. Doherty
Executive Vice President
Lebhar-Friedman, Inc.

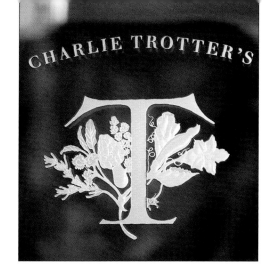

AWARDS

AAA Five Diamond 1993-present

Mobil Five Star 1996-present

Chicago Tribune—four stars

Crain's Chicago Business—four forks

Relais & Châteaux
Relais Gourmand 1995-present

James Beard Foundation
Outstanding Restaurant Award 2000
Outstanding Chef Award 1999
Who's Who in Food & Beverage Award 1996
Outstanding Wine Service 1993
Best Chef, Midwest, 1992

Restaurants and Institutions
Fine Dining Ivy Award 1990

Nation's Restaurant News
Fine Dining Hall of Fame 1991

Wine Spectator
Best Restaurant in the United States 2000
Best Restaurant in the World for Wine and Food 1998
Grand Award 1993-present

Traditions & Qualité
Les Grandes Tables du Monde 1998-present

Frederick Wildman & Sons
Moreau Award for Excellence in the Culinary Arts

Charlie Trotter personally takes charge of his elegant restaurant almost every night of the year.

CHAPTER ONE

A TRUE CHICAGO ENTREPRENEUR

Five nights a week, the man described as the Michael Jordan of American cooking holds court in his temple of culinary delight in Chicago's tony Lincoln Park neighborhood. Like basketball's Jordan, Charlie Trotter is in a league of his own. Named the nation's best chef at the 1999 James Beard Foundation Restaurant Awards, Trotter says, "I don't want to be the best at what I do. I want to be the *only* person who does what I do."

He just may be. Trotter's five-star eponymously named restaurant is one of a kind. The meticulously crafted dishes that emerge from his kitchen are works of art that happen to be on a plate. The wine service, masterfully paired with the food, is nonpareil. (Larry Stone and Joseph Spellman, the only two Americans ever to have won the world sommelier competition, both worked here.) Service is gracious and knowledgeable, and the ambience in the converted two-story 1908 brownstone has a luxurious feel. "We want to do something here that is completely unique," says the chef-owner, who studied political science at the University of Wisconsin before he discovered his true calling.

Like Jordan, Trotter is attentive to every phase of his game. "The paradigm is the pursuit of excellence for the cuisine, the ambience, the wine program, and the service—all in equal measure," he explains. "No one of those elements is more important than another."

His virtuosity is evident in the bustling state-of-the-art kitchen where he positions himself at the expediter's post, inspecting every dish. He briskly wipes the slightest hint of a smudge from the plates before they're whisked away by the waitstaff to the oohs and aahs of patrons, who pay an average of $135 per person, not including tax and tip.

Trotter barks orders and offers suggestions to the team of 16 chefs who execute his ingenious creations. He has a deep appreciation for jazz, and like jazz, his cuisine springs from the moment. This improvisation makes the cuisine, which reflects touches of traditional French cooking and Asian minimalism, hard to describe but easy to digest.

Wine Spectator, which likened Trotter to Jordan because both have one-of-a-kind moves, wrote that "no other U.S. chef can combine so many elements so seamlessly into a complex cuisine that somehow fits today's preferences for lightness and elegance as comfortably as a velvet robe and slippers."

Trotter puts it more succinctly: "The cuisine is the product of my personal tastes. It's simply what I like to eat." And he never cooks the same meal twice.

Trotter's key to putting his 90-seat restaurant on the map is pristine foodstuffs served at the height of their season. His flavors are true and explosive and are never masked with heavy

■

When they were at the restaurant, Master Sommeliers Joseph Spellman (left) and Larry Stone helped Trotter gain a following among wine-lovers.

Alert service is a hallmark of the Trotter's dining experience.

creams or sauces. Every night, he and his supporting cast prepare three tasting menus: a vegetable menu; a grand menu; and the *pièce de résistance*, the kitchen table menu.

A six-course grand menu might include such entrées as seared Maine diver scallops with kumamoto oyster sauce and braised kohlrabi; ragout of squab, rabbit saddle and lamb tongue with caramelized cauliflower and black truffle emulsion; and Summerfield Farm organic veal loin with savory date preserve, roasted garnett yams, and bok choy with Piedmont Black truffles.

In recent years, the Trotter brand has been extended to a handful of entrepreneurial forays that help pay for things the restaurant's budget normally wouldn't allow. "I have a terrible habit of spending money on the wine, the food, and the kitchen," Trotter says, noting that a 1995 remodeling of his kitchen cost $750,000. The studio kitchen where his TV program is produced ran about $350,000.

While Trotter's budding culinary empire has begun to spread its wings, the restaurant has not forsaken its homespun touches and its family roots. Dona-Lee Trotter, the chef's mother, serves as a tour guide on weekends, escorting guests through the kitchen and the restaurant's three wine cellars. His wife, Lynn, plays a similar role, and despite his growing superstar status, Trotter is at the helm of his restaurant nearly every night. Employees, who often put in grueling 14-hour days, invariably cite the restaurant's family orientation as part of their package of benefits.

"The cuisine is simply what I like to eat."
—*Charlie Trotter*

CHARLIE TROTTER'S MOVABLE FEAST

Charlie Trotter admits that his restaurant "lives beyond its means," primarily because of its generous employee benefits, an unusually large complement of chefs, and the cost of maintaining a million-dollar wine collection and a kitchen stocked with quality foodstuffs. Fortunately, he has been so successful with his side ventures that he doesn't have to worry.

A good example is the agreement he signed in 1997 with Philadelphia-based Aramark, a $6-billion corporate-catering concern. Trotter wrote a series of special menus that Aramark offers to clients who are looking for a grander dining experience when they host dinners, receptions, and other corporate events. Aramark managers and chefs also spend time in the kitchen watching Trotter and his team operate with surgical precision.

In the spring of 1999, Trotter signed on as a celebrity chef for United Airlines, which bills itself locally as "Chicago's Hometown Airline." Thus, first- and business-class passengers on United's Europe-bound flights are treated to such Trotteresque fare as Maine lobster with black pepper and vanilla bean vinaigrette; sea bass with bacon-sherry vinaigrette, braised leeks, and quinoa; and Thai-barbecued poussin with braised collard greens and preserved red onions. While haute cuisine and airline food might seem diametrically opposed, Trotter maintains that he can bring a touch of class to dining aloft.

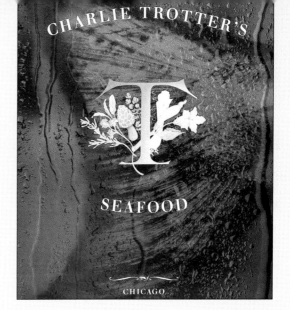

Trotter worked with United Airlines' executive chef Eric Kopelow to create in-flight menus. Among Trotter's other outside ventures, cookbooks (above, right) have been most successful.

Cookbooks have been an unexpected source of profit. Judi Carle, the restaurant's controller, who doubles as the general editor, says that the books were conceived as break-even propositions but have proved to be hot sellers. *The Kitchen Sessions with Charlie Trotter,* released in 1999, sold 80,000 copies in the first two months, and sales are projected to top 150,000. Trotter's popular TV series of the same name, aired on the Public Broadcasting Service (PBS), undoubtedly helps the cause, and being named America's best chef doesn't hurt sales either. Although Trotter won't confirm the figure, publishing sources estimate that the line of seven cookbooks contributes some $200,000 a year to the restaurant's bottom line.

Another venture is a line of specialty foods manufactured and distributed by Charlie Trotter Foods. The foods include such things as entrée sauces, dessert sauces, and smoked salmon.

Mark Signorio, the restaurant's director of special projects, says Trotter is approached almost weekly with offers for product endorsements and joint ventures. Nearly all are rejected, however, because they are not consistent with the Trotter brand.

Courtesy United Airlines, Kazlaw-Nelson

For his part, Trotter says that the best thing about starting his own restaurant was that it allowed him to work side-by-side with his father, Bob, who died in 1993 at the age of 64. The senior Trotter was a self-made millionaire in the executive recruiting field who imparted valuable lessons of entrepreneurship and business management to his son.

Although he had a dim view of the restaurant business, Bob Trotter didn't hesitate to bankroll his then 27-year-old son's business and to help run it. "My father always advised me to follow my dream," Trotter recalls fondly. "I was told I could be whatever I wanted to be so long as I was the best at what I did."

From his father, Trotter inherited an exemplary attention to detail. "I used to be a perfectionist, but I now realize that perfectionism isn't that interesting," he says. "I guess I'm an *excellentist,* if there is such a word." Not satisfied, Trotter expands on the concept: "It is more interesting to do things with sincerity and a certain quirkiness. With perfectionism there's no tolerance for failure, and failure is much more enlightening than success. While the successes are great, I've had innumerable failures but I've never let them defeat me. I just use them as points from which to push myself forward."

◼

Decor is deliberately understated so as not to compete with the food and the wine.

Photograph © Tim Turner

GATHERING AROUND THE KITCHEN TABLE

An institution preserved by moving the furniture two inches.

The kitchen table at Charlie Trotter's is the most coveted dining spot in Chicago. It has been host to countless gourmets, curious diners, Hollywood glitterati, politicians, and even royalty. (The King of Sweden, Carl Gustaf XVI, accompanied by a 24-man security detail that included a team of antiterrorist sharpshooters, broke bread here in 1997.) The table is Trotter's tip of the cap to the great French chefs who entertain guests in their kitchens.

The attraction is a 12-course, three-hour feast served at a table that turns over twice nightly only steps from Trotter's kitchen command post. In keeping with Trotter's philosophy, the food is light but the price is a hefty $150 per plate. Wine, tax, and tip are extra.

In 1995 the kitchen table became the source of controversy when city health inspectors considered shutting it down because they feared that disease could be spread if a sick diner were seated in the kitchen. Such a move could have drained more than $400,000 annually from the restaurant's revenue, and Trotter initially responded by threatening to start anew in California's Napa Valley.

But the city had bitten off more than it could chew. Trotter called in the local and national media to see the "health hazard" he was accused of creating. Impressed with the kitchen's immaculate appearance and the steps Trotter had taken to ensure his diners' safety, the media issued the restaurant a clean bill of health. Letters of support poured in from loyal patrons.

In the end, Trotter agreed to move the table about two inches farther away from the cooking area, and the festive banquets resumed. Subsequently, the restaurant and its famous chef have had to field even more requests for the best seat in the house.

■

Amid kitchen clamor, lucky guests concentrate on the meal of their lives.

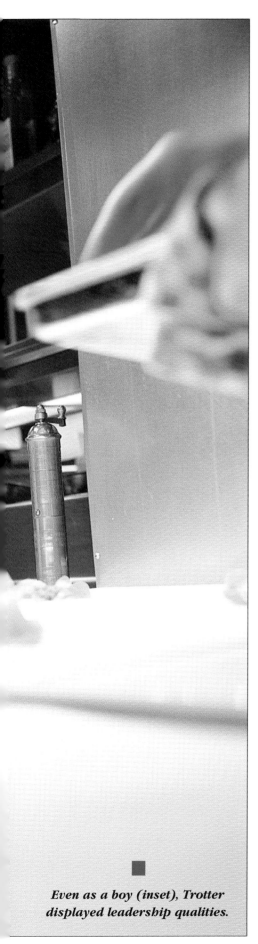

Even as a boy (inset), Trotter displayed leadership qualities.

CHAPTER TWO

NOT BAD FOR A KID WHO DIDN'T COOK

f someone had told Dona-Lee Trotter that her son Charlie, born in 1959, would one day become the nation's top chef, she probably would not have believed it.

"Charlie had no interest in cooking when he was growing up," says his mother. "He loved sports, like gymnastics and baseball. He was busy with his paper route, and he was always organizing activities for his younger sister and two younger brothers."

While he was growing up in Wilmette, a prosperous suburb on Chicago's North Shore, Charlie never expressed a strong preference for a particular career, but that didn't bother Bob and Dona-Lee Trotter. "We always encouraged our kids to follow their hearts," says Dona-Lee. She is not surprised, however, that Charlie quickly rose to the top of his profession: "He had a strong drive at everything he did."

After graduating from New Trier East High School, where he was a star trampolinist on the gymnastics team, Trotter enrolled at the University of Wisconsin, majoring in political science. Although he was still undecided about a career, he was certain that he would not go into the executive search business with his father. "My father discouraged me from even thinking about taking over his firm," recalls

*Dona-Lee Trotter at work. Although her oldest son's early interest in food was largely decorative (right),
she knew he would succeed at whatever he decided to do.*

Photograph © Steinkamp/Bellogg

Trotter. "Frankly, I never considered it. My father said I would never be fulfilled in life if all I did was take up where someone had left off. He told me that I needed my own set of challenges and failures, for better or for worse."

The seeds of entrepreneurship were planted in Charlie Trotter from an early age. "That was part of my motivation," he recalls. "My father said that I should seek the kind of opportunity that would allow me to be my own boss, to create my own destiny. And even if I failed, I would at least have done it on my own terms."

From his parents, Trotter also inherited a sense of noblesse oblige. "Giving time and money to charitable organizations was very important to them," says the young entrepreneur, who has helped raise hundreds of thousands of dollars for a variety of charities with his cooking demonstrations and speeches.

To earn extra spending money in college, Trotter waited tables and tended bar in a couple of casual restaurants in the college town of Madison. "That's when I got the bug for the restaurant life," he says. "I was impressed with the energy level, the dynamism you see in restaurants."

About the same time, Trotter began experimenting with basic dishes that he served to his friends and roommates. He started out by making lasagna, chili, and soup. In his book *Gourmet Cooking for Dummies,* Trotter describes his nascent efforts in the kitchen: "Although I started out with simple survival cooking, I soon realized how much fun I was having and decided to pursue cooking further. So I went out and bought several cookbooks and started to try many different types of dishes. Some turned out great, but others were, well. . . . So maybe I used a whole bulb of garlic in the veal scallopini instead of a clove. And it probably would have been better if I had figured out before the fire department arrived that blackened fish meant to blacken the spices, not the ceiling in my kitchen."

PORTRAIT OF A MAN WHO HAS FOUND HIS CALLING

When *Chicago* magazine described her husband as one of the meanest people in Chicago, Lynn Trotter believed the magazine got it only half right. "As a chef, Charlie can be one tough bastard," she says. "But he is also the most generous person on the planet." Known in the community for his fund-raising benefits for the underprivileged, Trotter shows his generosity on a personal level, too, his wife asserts. When an employee in a financial pinch approaches him for help, Trotter is quick to extend a loan.

"He's really a sweetheart, a soft-touch," says Lynn, who explains that one of her most important roles at the restaurant is to serve as a sounding board. "I have never met a person with such vision, but sometimes when he has a brainstorm, I play the devil's advocate and try to rein him in."

She recalls at least one occasion when she was *not* successful, however. Trotter had decided it would be wise to focus on the restaurant's superb wine service by eliminating hard liquor, and Lynn told him he could be making a big mistake. She argued that older members of the restaurant's clientele who enjoy a highball might look elsewhere. "But he did it anyway," she says, "and it worked."

In addition to his extraordinary vision, Lynn says her husband has succeeded "because he's poured his guts and his soul into the business. He is very lucky to have found his calling." Asked if she envisions their son filling his father's shoes some day, she says she hopes Dylan chooses a challenging profession, such as law or medicine—one that doesn't demand the long hours of operating a restaurant.

By the time he completed his degree in political science, Trotter was convinced that he would be a restaurateur. "I wanted to go into the field and see what was happening," he says. "I had discovered something I loved, and I was ready to pursue my dream."

He served as an apprentice for more than three years in some 20 restaurants in this country and abroad before returning to Chicago, where he and his father began laying the groundwork for the restaurant that would bear his name. The pair worked with architects, consultants, and construction contractors to ensure that every detail met their specifications. For about a year prior to the opening of the restaurant, Trotter catered dinner parties for business and social leaders in Chicago. The experience allowed him to begin applying some of the lessons learned during his immersion in the culinary arts, which had taken him from San Francisco to Paris and several places in between.

Trotter benefited significantly by combining his knowledge of food and wine with his father's business savvy. "I almost feel that I got an MBA through osmosis just by working with my father," he says. "I was exposed to someone who had an absolute eye for detail." He was 27 when the restaurant served its first meal in August 1987, and the father-son combination clicked from the start.

Unfortunately, not everyone in the Chicago culinary community was enthusiastic about the city's newest restaurant. "There was mumbling around town

Two of Trotter's keen interests: Running marathons (left) and making sure that his guests can choose from a wide selection of fine wines.

about some rich kid whose father paid for everything to help him start a restaurant, but I didn't let that bother me," says Trotter. "I believe that if you have opportunities in life, it's your obligation to realize them to the fullest."

Today, Trotter lives with his wife, Lynn, and their son, Dylan, in Chicago's stately Lincoln Park neighborhood, not far from the restaurant. Unlike most middle-aged chefs, who have grown flaccid from years of tasting their own handiwork, the five-foot-eight Trotter is fit and trim thanks to a regimen of jogging and calisthenics. He marked his 40th birthday by running a marathon in Bordeaux, France. The athletic discipline he learned as a youth has helped him stay in peak condition, he believes, because cooking is a sort of athletic event requiring a great deal of stamina. As if to underline the point, his glass-walled office is equipped with a six-foot-high basketball hoop at which he occasionally takes aim for diversion.

At home, he says he rarely cooks. "My problem is that I'm not home very much," says Trotter, who helps himself to his wife's tasty leftovers on his days off. For breakfast, he will prepare nothing more elaborate than eggs and toast for himself. He doesn't care for fast food, but will occasionally give in to his son's pleas for a trip to McDonald's.

The bespectacled Trotter, who is generally serious to the point of appearing cerebral, nevertheless has a wry sense of humor. One of his waiters, who joined the restaurant from a top Chicago steak house, says that when they pass each other in the kitchen Trotter teases him by growling, "Medium rare!" "Well done!" or "Rare!"—steak house terms that have no place in Trotter's more precise lexicon.

Trotter is an aficionado of jazz and film, and his literary tastes range from Saint Augustine to Dostoevski to gonzo journalist Hunter S.

Origins of a great chef: Trotter family (opposite, top) with Charlie at right, next to his father, Bob. Cooking up a storm in college and, above, a 1990 report in **Bon Appétit.**

Thompson. He sprinkles his conversations with references to movies, music, politics, and literature.

As his restaurant has evolved, Trotter has quietly adjusted his role there. In the early days, he says he was strictly "chef-creator. I was very hands-on with everything. Things have slowly evolved to the point where I play two distinct roles. You could say chef-entrepreneur is my daytime role. My nighttime role is hands-on chef-operator."

His day typically begins at noon and ends at about 1 a.m. But there are many days when he is in his office as early as 8:30 a.m. working on various entrepreneurial projects, such as developing his branded products or preparing the content of his cookbooks and TV programs. At 5 p.m., he dons a chef's jacket to oversee the activities in the kitchen. His only comment about the long hours: "I don't really see this as work, because I love what I do so much."

Fortunately, Trotter has been able to arrange his life so that he spends less time on the road than he did several years ago. Travel days are Sunday and Monday, when the restaurant is closed. "I used to travel three weekends out of four," he says. "Today, it's about once every three weeks." He prides himself on being in his restaurant about 240 of the 250 days it is open.

It is all part of his feeling that creating exquisite meals night after night is bound to have a ripple effect far beyond the walls of his restaurant. "We want to effect some good by making an aesthetic, cultural, and social contribution to the community," he says. "It wouldn't be any fun if we just made money for the hell of it."

Trotter family at ease: Lynn, Dylan, and Charlie enjoy some time to themselves.

"I believe that if you have opportunities in life, it's your obligation to realize them to the fullest."

How a Master Learned His Craft

The culinary education of Charlie Trotter began humbly. After graduating from the University of Wisconsin, he returned to his Wilmette, Illinois, home and began waiting tables at Sinclair's in nearby Lake Forest, where famed chef Norman Van Aken ran the kitchen. After several months of running food, he had the chance to begin preparing it when there was an opening for a line cook. "From my first day in the kitchen, it was clear that this was the life for me," he says. "There was no looking back. I had made the right decision."

Trotter had to explain to his father, Bob, that cooking was not some passing fancy. "I told him that my goal was to open my own restaurant," Trotter recalls, "and even though he could not understand why I was attracted to the restaurant business, he promised to help me financially. He told me, 'Whenever you are ready.'"

The younger Trotter realized he was a long way from being ready. His self-education in the restaurant business had several years and many miles to go. He moved to San Francisco, where he lived spartanly for a year and a half in a one-room apartment. He attended the California Culinary Academy, but, restless and driven, he dropped out after only four months. He remained in the city for several kitchen stints, including one at the Hotel Meridien, and he took full advan-

tage of San Francisco's proximity to the Napa Valley, where his appreciation of wine intensified during frequent forays into the wine country.

From San Francisco, Trotter moved to Jupiter, Florida, where he joined Van Aken and fellow chef Gordon Sinclair at a new restaurant called Sinclair's North American Grill. After six months in the kitchen, Trotter decided it was time for finishing school. "I thought I would go to New York or Paris to dine in some of the great restaurants," he says. "I went to New York a couple of times, but the experience wasn't as overwhelming as I had hoped it would be."

Trotter then set his sights on Paris, where, rather than working in a kitchen, he spent six months eating at some of the city's leading restaurants to get a taste of traditional French cooking. All the while, he immersed himself in the lives of the great chefs and read their cookbooks. "I knew that this was the final outing for me," he recalls. "Once I started my own restaurant, I would no longer be able to visit places like Paris."

It was several hundred miles from Paris, however, where Trotter had his watershed dining experience. His epiphany took place in 1985 at Girardet, the restaurant in Crissier, Switzerland, where the genius chef Fredy Girardet presided until his retirement in 1996. Trotter says there came a moment when "the atmosphere, the food, the wine, and the service all came together. At Girardet, I realized that enough was enough. It was time to bear down on my dream."

Business was brisk, even from the beginning.
Longtime friend Norman Van Aken (inset, right)
showed up for opening night.

CHARLIE TROTTER'S

CHAPTER THREE

A CLASSIC RIGHT FROM THE START

Charlie Trotter's vision of what his first restaurant would look like was inspired by some of the stately brownstone restaurants he had visited in New York City. "You could walk right up to one and not even realize it was a restaurant," he says.

Trotter also knew that he wanted his restaurant to be in the city. "Considering what we wanted to do with the food and the whole dining experience, it was necessary to be in an area with high population density and a high proportion of business travelers," he says. "And the most sophisticated dining clientele is here in the city."

Trotter and his father, Bob, who at that time was his business partner, looked at about 40 homes in Chicago that had the potential for conversion into a restaurant. But almost all of them were in residential zones where food and liquor could not be sold. Only two of the houses, it turned out, were in districts that would allow a commercial establishment.

Had the house that Trotter selected in the Lincoln Park area been a few feet farther west, the seven-month, $1.3-million renovation of the building would never have taken place. In Chicago, a business that sells liquor cannot be closer than 90 feet to a house of worship. What was soon to become Charlie Trotter's was 100 feet from the Greater

Little Rock Baptist Church on West Armitage.

The building was a two-story single family home built in 1908. By 1987, the neighborhood, about four miles northwest of Chicago's Loop, was in the throes of gentrification. Less than ten years before, many of the homes and apartments had been dilapidated, and a number of gangs had plied the turf.

Trotter's newly acquired building was gutted, leaving only the outer walls. "It looked like a Hollywood stage front," recalls Trotter. "The floors were gone; the piping and the wiring were all ripped out." But even in that state, he could sense the energy on that street and the great things that would soon be cooking inside.

Customers wasted no time in beating a path to Charlie Trotter's door once the restaurant was launched. "We were busy from day one," says Trotter of those early, exhilarating days of his dream restaurant. Driving the initial growth was the natural curiosity among diners about a hot new restaurant with prices that attracted both gourmet and bargain diners.

"We were offering a $60-per-person dining experience that we were selling for $30 to $35," he says. "We took a beating for a while. In fact, we lost money for the first 20 months of operation. We slowly began to raise our prices, and eventually we were making pretty good money." Over the years, the number of seats has been increased from 68 to 90.

Positive reviews and articles about the new restaurant also fed the early growth, says Trotter, who considers himself fortunate to have received good

Photographer: Jesse Walker

Although the restaurant has grown over the
years, the atmosphere is still intimate.

WHAT'S IN A NAME?

As the first day of business approached for his new restaurant in 1987, Charlie Trotter was still wrestling with what to call the place. "I had another name in mind," he recalls. "I just thought Charlie Trotter's sounded too egotistical. But a marketing consultant we were working with convinced me to put my name on the door."

The consultant argued that the chef's name should be featured in the same spirit as that of such great European chefs as Fredy Girardet, whose eponymously named restaurant in Crissier, Switzerland, was considered by Trotter to be at the culinary pinnacle. The consultant told Trotter, "You are going to be in the kitchen preparing your person-

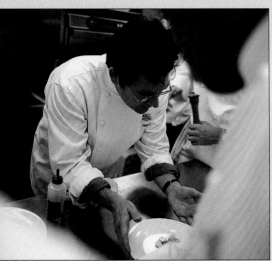

al cuisine, you've been working on every detail with the designers and the architect, and you'll be doing everything from sweeping the kitchen floor to putting the chairs up at night in the dining room."

The reserved, bespectacled Trotter, whose name has become synonymous with fine dining, says, "I'm not necessarily happy we used the name, nor do I have any regrets about it. Certainly, my personality is very much involved with the restaurant."

Trotter understood that there would be greater pressure and responsibility if his name and the restaurant's were the same. "There's more of an expectation that people should see you there in the kitchen or the dining room," he says. "I have found that when I am able to spend a few minutes at a table, it can make an evening seem more special."

These days, Trotter admits he's unable to spend much time in the dining room, except occasionally to peek in and look things over. "When I get a request to come out, I will honor it, but maybe not at that moment. Sometimes the waiter will bring the guests into the kitchen, and I'll say hello there."

■

Because his name is on the door, people expect Trotter to be on the scene.

CHARLIE TROTTER'S

press early on. He also believes his fledgling operation deserved the good reviews. "Some restaurants complain that it's not fair for critics to review them within the first six months of their opening. But I've always believed that if you're going to open your doors and charge diners full price, there should not be a grace period. Why should a restaurant learn at the public's expense?"

John Mariani, *Esquire* magazine's food critic, named Charlie Trotter's one of the top new restaurants of 1988. He mentioned the restaurant in the same breath with such Chicago dining landmarks as Carlos, the Everest Room, and Le Francais, all restaurants that Trotter sought to emulate. In his review of the nation's best new restaurants, Mariani wrote that Charlie Trotter's "pays homage to French classicism wedded to American ingenuity."

Menus in the first three years of the restaurant were à la carte. During the transition period, the menu was a combination of à la carte and a multi-course tasting or degustation menu. Trotter uses a musical analogy to explain his rationale for the

■

For Trotter, working with his father, Bob (shown above in pre-restaurant days), was equivalent to attending business school.

"Nobody is getting comfortable here," says Trotter. "We're always pushing it."

From the start, Trotter's was likened to the best restaurants in the country.

switch to a tasting menu. He notes that when people go to the symphony they are not expecting to hear a little of this or a little of that but rather long, elegantly composed strains of music.

As the restaurant matured and its prices rose, the bargain diners began to drift away and the dining room came to be dominated by gourmet diners and business travelers. Inspired by the French tradition, the restaurant established a chef's table in the kitchen so that guests could observe Trotter and his culinary acrobatics.

By the early 1990s, the restaurant's gourmet reputation began to spread beyond Chicago. It won an Ivy Award of Distinction in 1990, and other awards and honors soon rolled in. Recognition included a Relais Gourmand citation from Relais & Châteaux and five stars from the *Mobil Travel Guide*.

In 1993, Trotter bought the unkempt brownstone building next door and renovated it. No restaurant seats were added, but the first floor featured a kitchen, and offices were created on the second floor. An enclosed passageway at the rear joined the buildings, and an exterior re-design helped meld them into what now looks like a single property.

In 1994, the first in a series of Trotter's seven cookbooks was released. The books have been well received by critics and consumers alike. A rising star on the celebrity chef circuit, Trotter found himself on the road speaking to schools and industry gatherings, meeting the press, and promoting his books. During one hectic three-month period in 1995, he reluctantly stayed away from his kitchen 21 nights while promoting his latest book. He has since scaled back his travel schedule.

Properly orchestrated, a degustation menu is like a symphony.

In 1994, Trotter opened a Charlie Trotter's in Las Vegas's MGM Grand Hotel, but it was shuttered in less than a year. A new management team took over the hotel and wanted the restaurant to move downscale. Trotter, who had signed a ten-year lease with the hotel, turned thumbs down. He exercised his buy-out clause and pulled up stakes, but not before receiving a rich payout.

The experience in Las Vegas has not soured Trotter on extending his brand name in other ventures, however. In fact, he rattled some food purists in 1997 when he wrote *Gourmet Cooking for Dummies,* which was described in a cover blurb as, "The fun and easy way to whip up gourmet meals in your own kitchen." Although he was accused of pandering to the masses, his profile soared in 1999 when he began hosting his own PBS Series, *The Kitchen Sessions with Charlie Trotter.* The restaurant spent $350,000 to create the studio kitchen where Trotter does the TV show and numerous cooking demonstrations. The adjoining studio dining room can accommodate up to 20 guests.

Trotter cannot point to a particular point when his restaurant made the grade. "I don't think it was one review or story that did it," he says. "It was an accumulation of things." And despite the impressive collection of accolades that have piled up for him and his restaurant, Trotter says there's no chance that he and his staff will rest on their laurels. "Nobody is getting comfortable or getting tired of what they're doing here. We're always pushing it and pushing it, finding ways to get to the next level."

For any kind of occasion, Trotter's style is simple but elegant.

CHAPTER FOUR

A PHILOSOPHY DRAWN FROM THE WORLD OF JAZZ

Charlie Trotter thinks cooking and jazz are as natural a combination as food and wine. His improvisational cooking style can be as whimsical and free-spirited as a saxophonist pursuing a playful muse. "I don't like to intellectualize the cooking process; it's intuitive, spontaneous, in the moment," says Trotter, whose father, an amateur trumpeter, named his firstborn after sax legend Charlie Parker.

Like a serious musician, Trotter is grounded in the principles of his craft. After graduating from college, he immersed himself in cookbooks by such greats as Julia Child and James Beard. He studied the recipes and culinary philosophy of Fredy Girardet, who then presided at Girardet in Crissier, Switzerland. Trotter describes it as "the greatest restaurant on the planet," and after dining there, he adopted it as his model for what was to come.

"Cooking is exactly like playing music," he says. "Once historical precedence and classical ideas are understood, the possibilities are limited only by the artist's imagination." It is no accident that Trotter's PBS series, *The Kitchen Sessions with Charlie Trotter,* leans heavily on a jazz theme. Each program is introduced with a riff of cool, brassy jazz. "It's about approaching cooking with the spontaneity of a jazz session," he says. "Miles Davis may have played 'Stella by Starlight' hundreds of times, but he played it differently each time. The same thing happens with a plate of food."

For all the complexity of his dishes and all the unexpected combinations of flavors (sample: New York State foie gras with ruby grapefruit), there's a certain simplicity to Trotter's style. In the cookbook that

"It is good to know that you are eating unadulterate
farmers and growers who are directly connected wi

complements the TV series, he emphasizes simple preparation methods. "Cooking is not really that difficult," he writes. In fact, it's more about love and touch and caring than about special techniques or magical recipes. It's about caring for and loving the foodstuffs you're working with."

Trotter's philosophy of spontaneity shines through in this passage from the book: "One time you might make a fruit tart with peaches, the next time with plums or apples. This time you might serve it with vanilla-tarragon ice cream, the next time with a curried yogurt sorbet. Today you may prefer to grill your fish, tomorrow to steam it."

By tweaking the balance or by adding an ingredient or flavor, an ordinary dish can suddenly become Trotteresque or, as he likes to put it, "one that will blow people away."

His menus flow from his improvisational bent. He says he simply asks himself, "What do I want to eat today? What ingredients do I want to use?" And his instincts apparently have served him well. Reservations at his restaurant need to be made three months in advance, and landing a spot at his storied kitchen table can take up to six months.

He has a passion for healthful, fresh foodstuffs, and he spares no expense in ensuring that they find their way into his kitchen. "The taste of free-range and organic products is so much better than the alterna-

■

The team behind the cuisine: Cooking is about caring for the foodstuffs you work with.

ood and supporting
ne land."—*Charlie Trotter*

FOR EVERY GREAT MEAL, THE PERFECT WINE

Robert Houde, the sommelier at Charlie Trotter's, expresses the restaurant's mission this way: "We are all here to allow customers to have the greatest dining experience they've ever had."

Houde's role in helping the restaurant achieve that lofty goal is critical, and decisions about how to pair the wine with the food can often be as spontaneous as Trotter's menus. A jazz pianist and vocalist in his spare time, Houde says his improvisational skills come in handy when he and Trotter attempt to orchestrate the perfect combination of wine and food selections: "I might, for example, go to the chef and say that I see the cuisine being served as a Sauvignon blanc dish, and he might say that he sees it as more of a Riesling. We'll just talk things out. There's often not a single right answer for any-thing, because there can be so many creative combinations."

Because Trotter's savory cuisine, though light, still has great intensity of flavor, Houde says the restaurant tends to favor wine from France's Burgundy region. The varietals "have a little more finesse," he observes. "They are not so tannic and gripping as to 'muscle up' a food."

While Burgundy predominates, wines from Bordeaux also have a strong presence on Charlie Trotter's list of 1,300 selections. Wines from the Rhone Valley, Alsace, and Champagne are well represented, too, as are selections from California, Australia, and Germany.

tive," he says emphatically. "It is good to know that you are eating unadulterated food and supporting farmers and growers who are directly connected with the land."

Another cornerstone of Trotter's culinary philosophy is explosive flavors; nothing is muted by heavy creams or sauces. He prefers saucing with vegetable-juice-based vinaigrettes and light, emulsified stocks and purées, as well as delicate broths and herb-infused meat and fish essences.

Like the foodstuffs he selects so carefully from his purveyors, Trotter is no less particular about the wine stocked in the restaurant's three redwood cellars, which are carefully controlled for temperature and humidity. Trotter believes that food and wine should not only complement each other but *inspire* one another. The interplay of wine and food is an integral part of the dining experience.

The food and wine, combined with the service and ambience, are designed to create "something that is absolutely unique for the customers," says Trotter. "The dining experience here can be appreciated by a seasoned, knowledgeable gourmet or by lay diners who may not come to a restaurant like this except as part of a perfect vacation, a 50th birthday party, or a 25th wedding anniversary. Regardless of who they are or why they are here, we must make this one of the best experiences of their life."

Wine Spectator concluded that Charlie Trotter's is doing just that. In 1998, the magazine's readers voted it Best Restaurant in the World for Wine and Food, and two years later they declared it Best Restaurant in the U.S. 2000.

With 1,500 wines to choose from, diners are sure to find just the right one for their meal.

"The pursuit of excellence is an
expensive proposition," says Trotter, whose
operational philosophy seems to be,
"If it ain't broke, then break it."

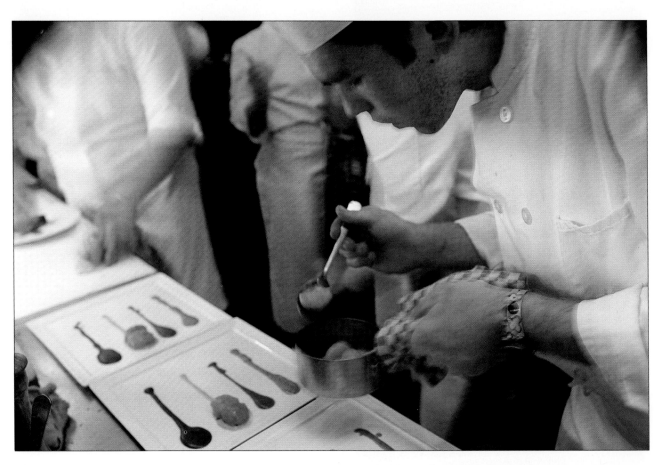

■

*Attention to detail is why
Trotter's is cited as one of the
world's great restaurants.*

All of the restaurant's wine is served in delicate
Riedel crystal stemware, which speaks to the respect
Trotter and his staff have for the wine. The downside
is that the stemware is so fragile that it doesn't stand
up to daily wear and tear. Stemware losses exceeded
$40,000 one year, but Trotter figures that's a small
price to pay for superlative wine service.

After all, the pursuit of excellence is an expensive
proposition, insists Trotter, whose operational philosophy seems to be, If it ain't broke, then break it.
Although the restaurant had a fine seven-year-old

"Do You Plan to Join Us Again?"

Charlie Trotter can quickly determine how well he and his team are doing. He does so informally by frequently asking customers if the food and service have met their expectations. But Trotter and company also gauge their performance scientifically. After the meal has been served, each table is presented with a customer-satisfaction survey that asks the diners to grade such elements as food, wine, and service. They are also invited to grade the evening, and they are asked if they plan to return to the restaurant. More than half the diners fill out the cards, which come complete with a stamp for those who want to mail in their surveys.

Patrons apply a ranking from 1 (poor) to 5 (outstanding) to such questions as "How would you rate the food?" "How would you rate the wine list?" and "How would rate your wait person?" They are invited to add a comment to each rating.

It was Trotter's business-savvy father, Bob, who instituted the customer-satisfaction survey, and it has become the restaurant's most valuable intelligence-gathering tool. Diners who answer no to the question "Do you plan to join us again in the future?" are asked to provide an explanation. An open-ended response is also requested to the question "What could we have done to improve your experience?"

As he riffles through a stack of the surveys on the table in his office above the restaurant's studio kitchen, Trotter says, "I read every one of the surveys that come in. I read the highlights and the low lights. I go over the comments and grades at every pre-service meeting and then divvy them up and give them to each waiter. If customers say they will not come back for any reason whatsoever, either I or my assistant will call them and invite them back as our guests. We have our hand absolutely on the pulse of the clientele."

While the feedback can be humbling at times, Trotter says that without it the restaurant could not possibly determine if it is living up to its goal of excellence. "It keeps us from getting comfortable with what we do," he says. "We see every day as a new opportunity to raise the bar."

*The customer-satisfaction survey is one
key to maintaining impeccable service.*

kitchen with magnificent equipment, Trotter ordered it ripped apart in early 1995. The walk-in cooler was replaced with under-the-counter and countertop refrigeration at each station. Fluorescent *and* incandescent lights were installed. (Incandescent lights were placed above the expediter's station, for example, so that Trotter could see a dish in the same light as the diner; what looks rare under fluorescent lamps might be revealed as medium rare under an incandescent light.)

When the dust had settled, Charlie Trotter's could boast one of the most up-to-date cooking facilities in the world. "For example, we replaced a ceiling that had already been replaced twice before," says Trotter. The ceiling is stainless steel and equipped with smoke-eating exhaust units to purify the air and eliminate airborne grime.

Trotter, described by one of his employees as a "clean freak," is fastidious about the condition of his kitchen. If it is immaculate, there's a good reason: Every night, it is scrubbed down by the chefs and the kitchen crew after the last guest has been served.

Obviously, the little things mean a lot here. "There was no logical reason to do something like that renovation," Trotter says. "It cost about $750,000, and it took us a couple of years to pay off." Although the immediate objective was to make the kitchen more efficient and ergonomically correct, he cites the renovation as an example of how his restaurant pushes the envelope toward excellence. "There is not only a constant rejuvenation and renovation of the physical property here but a sense of reinvention with everything we do," he says. "The reinvention process seems very natural to us, and we put our performance under the microscope each day."

Everyone pitches in to help with the cleanup ritual at the end of the evening.

Trotter's food reflects a variety of culinary influences.
Above, Stuffed Breast of Organic Chicken with Braised Oxtail, and Poached
Foie Gras with Consommé and Cabbage. (Charlie Trotter's Meat and Game)

CHAPTER FIVE

AN ORIGINAL AMERICAN CUISINE

Charlie Trotter's cuisine has been described as cutting-edge, complex, ornate, extravagant, picaresque, exotic, even poetic. But Trotter sees his culinary handiwork in far simpler terms: "It's the combination of flavors and textures that are put together in a way not seen before."

The largely self-taught chef says his style defies easy categorization. "The food has elements of the great tradition of French cuisine, but there is also a distinct Asian, minimalist aesthetic to it," he says. "There is less fat and a strong vegetable influence."

Trotter is passionate about vegetables, and one of his long-range goals is to open an all-vegetable restaurant in the Chicago area. "I have always considered vegetable cookery the most interesting part of cuisine," he writes in his 1996 cookbook, *Vegetables*. "Vegetables provide an incredible depth and complexity in both flavor and texture, not to mention an extraordinary range of colors and shapes that cannot be matched by beef or salmon. I must confess though, I am far from a vegetarian. I just happen to be in love with the experience of touching, cooking, and eating the multitude of vegeta-

bles, fruits, legumes, and grains. It is sincerely one of
the most sensual joys of my life."

True to his improvisational nature, Trotter has no
signature dishes. After all, he would have to make the
dish more than once to be considered signature, and
that's not his style. Over the course of more than 12
years and 3,000 nights of service, the restaurant has
produced an astounding 12,000 distinct menus.
Individual dishes and desserts are too numerous to
count. Trotter claims to be equally proud of each of his
creations, and he has enshrined a number of them in a
series of cookbooks.

From *Vegetables* come two dishes that reflect his
eclectic tastes. The first has Asian overtones, and the
second echoes both European and American influences:

■ Ragout of baby bok choy, haricots verts, yellow
wax beans, and dragon's tongue beans with Japanese
cucumber sauce;

■ Blood oranges with warm braised Belgian endive,
Missouri black walnuts, and Gorgonzola.

Jeff Yankelow, a chef who joined Charlie Trotter's in
1997 at age 23, recalls being overwhelmed by the cor-
nucopia of exotic foodstuffs that flows through the
kitchen door from all points of the globe. "We get so
much fish from Japan and other parts of the world," he
says. "We get to work with product that has just been
taken out of the sea, and we clean it from start to finish.
You learn something new about food every day here."

In the early days of the restaurant, the dishes were
more substantial and the number of courses for dinner
was twice what it is today. *Esquire*'s food critic, John
Mariani, wrote in 1995 that "Trotter's gargantuan 12-
course dinners have been cut to a quite digestible six."

*The dining experience at
Charlie Trotter's consists of a
series of petite courses.*

Trotter takes pride in coming up with new combinations of flavors and textures.

The 12-course meal still reigns at the restaurant's single table in the kitchen, but the six-course tasting, or degustation, menu is the rule in the restaurant's three, 30-seat dining rooms. Diners choose from either the grand menu (sample dish: slow-roasted Scottish salmon with Mountain Island flat oysters, oyster emulsion, truffled potatoes, and kohlrabi); or the vegetable menu (sample dish: roasted organic root vegetables served in a deconstructed format with legume sauces and pearled barley).

The fare at Charlie Trotter's is always evolving. "Over the years, the cuisine has become lighter, more streamlined, more minimalist," says Trotter. "I love things in small packages. We're emphasizing fewer and fewer notes, two or three items on a plate, like a piece of braised endive, a piece of caramelized apple, a little emulsion of red wine. That's it."

His dishes are things of beauty, featuring precise cuts of, say, organic game and other ingredients arranged like colorful jewels on dazzling pieces of china. They seem almost other-worldly.

Desserts are treated with the same degree of respect as the savory cuisine. No meal is complete, says the boss, "without a sweet thing or two at the end." Putting an exclamation point on a perfect meal is the job of Michelle Gayer and her four pastry chefs.

"Restaurants that want to cut corners do so in the pastry department, but not here," says Gayer. "[The restaurants] might order really great mushrooms, for example, but the pastry chef is not allowed to order really great chocolate. Or some restaurants won't provide the pastry chef any assistants, which means at night the desserts might be prepared by someone from another department."

INFLUENCES FROM AROUND THE WORLD

*C*harlie Trotter's cuisine is global. His pristine, seasonal foodstuffs are supplied by more than 50 top-quality purveyors throughout the world. The food is "a melting pot of many world cuisines that are melded together to create something entirely new," says chef de cuisine Matt Merges, noting that until now American cooking has been characterized by strong French and Italian influences. Merges says he feels at home in Charlie Trotter's kitchen where one of the goals is to "push yourself and your team in terms of inventing a truly American cuisine."

To inform his cooking, Merges travels the world. "I have been to China, Japan, and throughout Europe," he says. "Our family vacations are very food-centered, because we value the importance of food and the farming culture." From each destination, Merges takes a bit away and introduces it at Charlie Trotter's.

Guests may enjoy either the Grand Menu or the Vegetable Menu, or they may simply leave it up to Chef Trotter to prepare a spontaneous menu.

Over the course of more than 12 years, the restaurant has produced an astounding 12,000 distinct menus.

"We want to do more than merely satisfy our customers. It has to be the best dining experience of their lives."—*David LeFevre, sous-chef*

As the guests marvel at the creations, they often ask who prepared a particular dish. "The fact is the dishes could be the product of sixteen chefs at night and four during the day operating under chef Trotter's vision," says sous chef David LeFevre. "A tremendous amount of work goes into it."

LeFevre, who studied industrial engineering at the University of Wisconsin before experiencing a change of heart and enrolling at the Culinary Institute of America, spent a year cooking in several restaurants in France. "I came to appreciate the wonderful traditions of French cooking," he says, "but their problem is they have blinders on when it comes to considering new foods."

That's hardly the case at Charlie Trotter's, where the kitchen is always open to fresh ideas and ingenious ways to incorporate new foods and techniques into the mix. "For example, by using organic soy sauce from Japan, you can bring a dish to a higher level," says LeFevre. The watchwords are "light," "minimalist," and "simple," he explains, adding that "the flavors are true; rather than heavy sauces, vinaigrettes are used so as not to mask the flavor."

Living up to Charlie Trotter's culinary standards isn't easy, says LeFevre. "We are on a pedestal right now, and every customer who comes in here expects a perfect meal. But you have to prepare them more than just the perfect meal, because we want to do more than merely satisfy them. It has to be the best dining experience of their life."

LeFevre (right) apprenticed at restaurants in France.

AND FOR DESSERT

Dessert at Charlie Trotter's is a grand affair, often ranging from four to six courses, and Michelle Gayer is responsible for making it all happen. The surest way to crown a meal is "by taking old, classic desserts and 'Trotterizing' them," says Gayer. "You do that by bumping it up with a new and different twist."

Some great restaurants treat dessert as an afterthought by finishing the meal "with a big slice of chocolate cake smothered in whipped cream," she says. "That really doesn't do the meal justice—and it doesn't happen at Charlie Trotter's."

Dessert recipes include such irresistible treats as strudel made with pumpkin, pecans, ginger, and caramelized apple and accompanied by maple syrup ice cream. Then there's the bing cherry brownie sundae with bittersweet chocolate and kona coffee sauce, and the pineapple-polenta upside-down cake with mango and caramel-lime ice cream.

Gayer has stitched together a network of top-quality purveyors "who know our reputation for wanting only the finest ingredients. They will call us, for example, only if they get an excellent batch of strawberries. We have that kind of relationship with our purveyors."

For Gayer, one of the key advantages to the menu at Charlie Trotter's is its flexibility. "We can change at any moment, [depending on] whatever comes in the door that day," she says. "If the pears aren't quite ready, we'll go with a fruit that is." Desserts at Charlie Trotter's, she says, are very fruit-oriented. They are designed to celebrate the glorious flavors of a perfectly ripe piece of fruit served at the height of its season.

There is a more exacting adherence to pastry recipes than with savory cuisine, but in true Trotter spirit Gayer enjoys plenty of latitude. For example, she and her dessert crew are ever conscious of the wine being served a guest as they prepare a dessert. "If someone has a bit of red wine left and they're not big on desserts, we might prepare them a cheese plate," she says. "It all depends on the individual diner and how the waiter reads the table." If the reading is correct, Gayer knows, she can send everyone home on a sweet, satisfied note.

A good dessert should do justice to a great meal. At right, nectarine confit with Château d'Yquem granita.

Sommelier Robert Houde helps guests with a wine selection.

CHAPTER SIX

POISED TO PROVIDE
AN UNFORGETTABLE DINING
EXPERIENCE

A meal at Charlie Trotter's is designed to be *the* transcendent dining experience, produced through a perfectly balanced orchestration of cuisine, wine, service, and ambience. "No one of those four elements do we consider more important than another," says Trotter.

Diners craving the complete dining experience will never encounter the word *no* while in the care of his attentive waitstaff, assures Trotter, whose restaurant has twice been voted the best restaurant in the world for wine and food by readers of *Wine Spectator*. "We believe there is no such thing as no here," he says. Indeed, he seems to have stolen a page from Nordstrom, the department store known for its never-say-never approach to customer service.

Trotter, who is known to answer the door, take out the garbage, and haul in deliveries during the day, recalls how two doctors, in Chicago for a convention, showed up on his doorstep one day around noon. "They had heard about the restaurant, and they wanted to have lunch," he says. "I had to tell them that we don't serve lunch." But he was so struck by their sincerity that he invited them in, seated them at the restaurant's famous kitchen table, and personally prepared their meal. The sumptuous lunch was on the

*Service is precise without
being regimented.*

There's a Midwestern
wholesomeness to the
treatment of the guests,
which is exactly how
Trotter wants it.

house, and the doctors returned to their convention true believers in the Trotter brand of hospitality.

Operations director Mitchell Schmieding, who trains and supervises the front-of-the-house staff, says a server is expected to do just about anything to "push a table over the edge" into the realm of complete satisfaction. For example, if a guest arrives in a harried state after a difficult day, the waitstaff know instinctively how to restore the guest's mood. When not running food or pouring wine, they position themselves at a discrete distance, watching the diners and trying to anticipate their needs.

Diners should leave Charlie Trotter's with the sense that their evening "wasn't just about the food," Schmieding says. "It's really about being well taken care of. It's an emotional exchange that they'll never forget. Unlike some restaurants that turn off the lights and pull up the flowers at the end of the evening, we make sure the last guest enjoys the same experience at 1 a.m. as the first guest did at 6 p.m."

There's a precision to the service provided by Charlie Trotter's team of dark-suited waiters as they deliver a parade of courses on exquisite china and patiently explain the provenance of each dish. The menus, which guests may take home, are like albums. They feature a color photo of a dazzling entrée on the cover. Inside, the evening's bill of fare is secured on each corner by beige ribbons.

TO INCREASE STATURE, THINK SMALL

Most businesses aim to attract more customers, not fewer. But Charlie Trotter is convinced that less is more, even though it may mean leaner revenues.

To serve customers in an even more personal manner, Trotter says the restaurant is gradually reducing the number of patrons. "We used to serve upwards of 200 guests on both Friday and Saturday nights," he says. "Now, it's closer to 160, and we'd like to get it to 120." He points out that driving down the number of covers per night sounds financially counter-productive, but he believes that in the long run, diners will appreciate the more attentive level of service and will be willing to pay for it.

Though precise, the service is never regimented or robotic. "Our style changes from table to table," Schmieding says. "It's all in how we read the guest; there are no rules." *Wine Spectator* wrote that Charlie Trotter's service "followed a classic pattern, never hovering, never hurried, but always on top of things. The general tone was quiet, poised, serene. All the excitement was on the plate or in the glass."

Despite the restaurant's reputation and the fact that a meal costs $100 before wine, tax, and tip, there is nothing snooty or intimidating about the service. There's a Midwestern wholesomeness to the treatment of the guests, which is exactly how Trotter wants it. Lay diners and gourmets alike are expected to feel comfortable at their tables, which are covered with white linen and topped by a small vase of flowers. After the meal, Trotter's mother, Dona-Lee, often lends a homespun touch, greeting the guests sweetly and guiding them through the restaurant's kitchens and wine cellars.

If the dining experience is enriched by thoughtful consideration, it also depends on tact and a keen assessment of human nature. Mindful that selecting a wine from an imposing list of some 1,200 vintages can seem daunting to even the most sophisticated gastronome, sommelier Robert Houde puts his disarming manner to good use. "I explain that I have tried all the wines and they have not," he says. "It's not a matter of someone being smarter than the other person. Most people don't have the time or money to sample 40 wines a day."

Houde says that he and the waitstaff "are constantly reading the customer, trying to get into their thoughts," to come up with an inspired suggestion for a wine from the million-dollar collection housed in Trotter's three state-of-the-art cellars. "When you find something that appeals to the diner, it lifts them

Guests enter Charlie Trotter's through a two-story atrium.

*Behind the scenes,
careful preparation and
an imposing selection of
wine (opposite).*

and carries them away," he says, describing the experience in almost spiritual terms.

The greatest pleasure in his job, says Houde, "is making a connection with the customers through the wine, regardless of whether it's a $30 bottle or a $10,000 bottle." He particularly enjoys getting people to explore vintages they had never thought of trying. "I figure they're already being adventurous with the menu, because they aren't quite sure what they'll encounter," he says. "It's the same with the wine list." Gesturing toward the dining room, he adds, "We have very intelligent people sitting here. When they realize they are in over their heads, they'll defer to us on a selection."

Although the wine service is primarily the responsibility of the waitstaff, Houde floats through the three dining rooms. At times, he will take charge of a table that has a complicated set of requests. If he has the slightest doubt about how to match the wine with the

■

A Study in Lady Apples.
(Charlie Trotter's Desserts)

cuisine, he repairs to the kitchen and confers with Trotter about designing an ideal progression of wines.

Timing is everything when it comes to superlative service, and the task of bringing things together on time falls to Ervin Sandoval, the restaurant's expediter. "I try to pace the tables from my post in the kitchen," says Sandoval, who started at the restaurant as a busboy soon after emigrating to the U.S. from his native Guatemala. "It's like putting a puzzle together every night."

As the liaison between the chefs and the waitstaff, Sandoval may have the toughest job in the house, for he knows that nothing can ruin an evening quicker than a dish served too late or too soon. Yet he seems unflappable on the firing line, handing off a steady stream of entrées and desserts to the hovering waiters. "At most restaurants the waiters call the food, but not here," says Sandoval, who works side-by-side with Trotter, making split-second determinations as to what goes where and when.

At Charlie Trotter's, the dining experience begins even before a guest steps into the restored 1908 brownstone. Special projects director Mark Signorio, who has a design degree from Chicago's School of the Art Institute, works closely with Trotter to create a welcoming atmosphere that literally begins at curbside. A row of pear trees lines the street, and the sidewalk is inlaid with red bricks. There is no sign, just a brass plaque on the side of the building that says "Charlie Trotter's." Some customers, expecting a more commercial facade, walk past before realizing they have missed Chicago's most celebrated restaurant.

The interior is as elegant and understated as the exterior. On entering, guests find themselves in the foyer bar, a lofty atrium outfitted in stately Viennese Biedermeier-style furnishings. Along one wall is a 20-

Ideally, says Mitchell Schmieding, diners will leave feeling that the evening wasn't just about food but about being cared for.

foot-tall wine rack, and across the room is a lithograph by German painter Joseph Muller entitled *Two Bathing Ladies*.

Banquettes line the main dining room on the first floor. A serving credenza displaying a colorful floral arrangement dominates the middle of the room, while elegant sconces accent the perimeter. Wainscoting and moldings of mahogany, custom-woven wall fabric, plush carpeting, and silk draperies all help to create an air of luxury. Similar motifs are employed in the second-floor balcony dining room and in the adjacent salon dining room. The latter is highlighted by a wall of bins displaying a portion of the restaurant's award-winning wine collection.

The minimalist approach to decor endows all the dining rooms with a quiet elegance. There are no statues or artwork. "The design of the rooms is purposely understated," explains Signorio. "The people and the food are the art, and the dining rooms are the canvas."

Not surprisingly, people rarely comment on the ambience (or lack of it) surrounding the most envied seat in the house. That seat is at the special table a few feet from Trotter's kitchen command post, where a well-choreographed frenzy unfolds every night beneath bright lights and stainless steel. Guests are pampered by their waiter as they spend three hours enjoying an astonishing 12-course meal under Trotter's watchful eye. Here, decor yields to delectation. As one diner exulted as she took her seat, "I've been waiting for this table for five years!"

Trotter's decor achieves a quiet elegance. In the foyer bar, guests are greeted by **Two Bathing Ladies** *(left).*

Mitchell Schmieding (second from left) helps direct traffic at the expediter's station.

CHAPTER SEVEN

FIELDING A TEAM THAT PUTS THE CUSTOMER FIRST

Although his name is on the door, Charlie Trotter is quick to point out that "this restaurant is not the product of me alone." It takes a staff of 50 to run the 90-seat restaurant five nights a week, 50 weeks a year. Melding and motivating the 22 staffers in the kitchen with the 22 in the front of the house and with the 6 office employees is one of Trotter's biggest challenges.

The team-building process begins with making smart hires. "We cherry-pick the best people from other restaurants," says Trotter. "They come from amazingly diverse backgrounds. Some have come from top-flight restaurants. Others come from midlevel restaurants, and others have virtually no experience."

Trotter is more impressed by a candidate's can-do attitude than by a résumé. "I'm looking for someone who can take excellence over the top," he says. "For example, I'm looking for the kind of person who won't think twice about pouring some extra champagne for a customer who has waited ten minutes for a table. A good server doesn't hesitate in that situation. He or she simply makes it happen."

It usually takes a new hire from six months to a year before he or she can make an impact on the restaurant, says Trotter. Not only does the new employee have to learn the system, but he or she must take every assignment seriously.

Trotter's team-building strategy:
Hire people with a can-do attitude.

LIKE A HARDY, ROUGH-AND-TUMBLE FAMILY

Executing the culinary vision of Charlie Trotter is a demanding game where every plate is expected to be a home run. Compounding the pressure is the close quarters in Trotter's intensely bright, tile-and-stainless-steel kitchen which crackles with the manic intensity of a big-city hospital emergency room.

It is an atmosphere that can push people to the limit. "There are times when we are fighting and arguing because of the pressure," says chef de cuisine Matt Merges. "It can get so emotional that people are crying because it is so hard."

Tempering the intensity, however, is the sense of belonging to a close-knit family of the best chefs in the business, says Merges. "We're like brothers and sisters who have their occasional disagreements in the heat of battle." The average age in the Trotter kitchen is 25, and the average tenure is one-and-a-half to two years. "There's a line in this business that the back door is never locked," says Merges, noting that his chefs are often targets of other restaurants that hope to add a touch of the Trotter mystique to their own menus.

To help reduce turnover, Merges instituted an end-of-evening meeting during which the entire kitchen crew is encouraged to unwind by sharing their impressions about what went wrong or right that night. Merges believes the meetings, which can last until 2 a.m. on weeknights and later on weekends, have built an esprit de corps. They are also an opportunity for Merges, who oversees all kitchen operations, to tell his crew how proud he is of their Herculean efforts. "I'm not saying we're great every time," he says, "but we're certainly aiming for greatness."

Trotter expects his employees to give up a good portion of their lives to the pursuit of excellence.

Mitchell Schmieding, the restaurant's director of operations, says the best training program in the world means little unless the employee is passionate about what he or she is doing. "We make some mishires, yes," he says, noting that those who fail to live up to the high standards at Charlie Trotter's are usually those who regard their position as just a job. "Some want to work here because this restaurant is such a monument, but it has to go beyond that."

The benefits package is a drawing card at Charlie Trotter's, where employees, including the waitstaff, are salaried. In a compensation plan unusual for the restaurant industry, Trotter's waitstaff are paid a salary from the pool of customers' gratuities. They make as much money as they would on the traditional tip system but without uneven nightly swings. They are also entitled to medical and dental coverage as well as a 401K savings plan. Trotter's compensation package is unusually generous in an industry where employees often must provide their own benefits. It engenders loyalty and provides employees with stability that allows them to make serious financial commitments, such as taking out a mortgage.

In return, not surprisingly, the restaurant's

Trotter's kitchen brigade with Guest Chef Tetsuya Wakuda (from Sydney).

*Rather than strict rules,
training emphasizes fostering
individual excellence.*

In hiring, Trotter seeks "the kind of person who won't think twice about pouring extra champagne for a customer who has waited for a table."

expectations of an employee are extraordinarily high. "If you've made an error, as little as it may be, there is the sense that you have let everyone down," says Schmieding, who joined the restaurant in 1988 and is one of the most senior employees. "It isn't that you have let me down, or you let Charlie down, or yourself down but that you've let a whole team down. We are very much a family here because we spend so much time together, often 12 to 14 hours a day. These are people you don't want to disappoint."

The concepts of family and the pursuit of excellence are emphasized during training, but employees looking for a set of rules to guide them won't find any. "In a sense, there are no rules," says Schmieding. "I can't remember ever saying no to any kind of reasonable customer request. If you sincerely care about a client, you'll find a way."

Schmieding feels strongly that attention to seemingly small details is what drives the restaurant's superlative service. "It's seeing that the napkin is changed if the customer gets up," he says, "or telling the kitchen to hold off on the food if the customer is away from their seat." Servers who don't have an immediate task are conditioned to "waiting in the weeds" so that they can jump in to assist a fellow server at a table that is not their own.

Even after the meal is over, servers are called upon to maintain the Trotter hospitality. "Toward the end of the evening, when customers are leaving, our service staff are out hailing cabs, assisting with the valet parking, or giving tours of the restaurant," says Schmieding. "No one disappears."

Paul Larson, the senior member of the waitstaff, says that a server "has a variety of tools to create an unforgettable dining experience for the customer."

For operations director Mitchell Schmieding (above, left), the secret is in the details.

A New Challenge Spawns A New Career

Sari Zernich wasn't sure she had the right stuff for Charlie Trotter's fast track. After working at a variety of cooking stations in the kitchen, she grew weary of the 12- to 14-hour days. With an eye toward capitalizing on her food-science degree from the University of Illinois, she applied for an opening at Chicago-based Quaker Oats Co.

But when she told Charlie Trotter of her plans to leave, he asked if she would consider taking on a new role at the restaurant. He needed help working on a cookbook that would be the second in a series of high-gloss cookbooks.

Zernich accepted the assignment and has never looked back. She hasn't had time. The books have been enormously successful, selling upwards of 70,000 copies each and providing a steady stream of revenue for the restaurant. *The Kitchen Sessions with Charlie Trotter,* for example, claimed the No. 1 spot on the Los Angeles Times Cookbook Hot List after its release in 1999.

Zernich, who works in the restaurant's front office, is responsible for recipe testing. In that capacity, she handles research and development for Trotter's cookbooks and for the Kitchen Sessions TV series. Because Trotter does the series without a script, Zernich captures his on-the-fly creations using a combination of Post-it notes, Polaroid photos, and quotes hastily typed into her laptop computer. With that information in hand, she and Judi Carle, a front-office colleague, piece together the recipes.

Carle, the restaurant's controller, points out that the cookbooks are an important part of the package that has become Charlie Trotter's. "The television doesn't produce revenue, because it's on PBS," she says, "but it does help sell the books, and the books help sell the reservations. After they've seen the show, it's not unusual for people to come to Chicago for no other reason than to eat." (The restaurant does not advertise, relying instead on publicity generated in local, trade, and national media.)

For Zernich, the books have been the basis of a new career. "I'm so happy I didn't take the job at Quaker," she says. "Charlie lets you run with the ball. He'll never tell you to stop. I think we all like to surprise him by showing him how far we can take a project. Sometimes little projects like that first cookbook turn into huge empires."

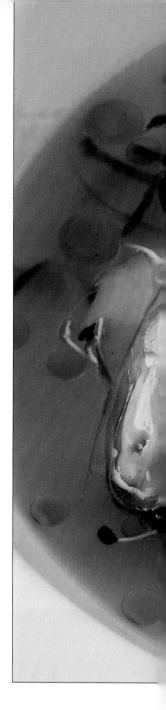

Steamed Gindai and Mussels
with Lemongrass Broth,
Braised Swiss Chard,
and Soba Noodles.
(Charlie Trotter's Seafood)

Larson, who joined Charlie Trotter's in 1991 after serving as maître d' at several top hotels, sometimes finds himself playing concierge for out-of-town diners. "I've made reservations for our customers at other restaurants many times," he says. "The moment the customer walks through the door, I'm responsible for their comfort. We do that by being knowledgeable and poised."

The quest for excellence so apparent in the front of the house is just as pronounced behind the scenes. Amid the kinetic atmosphere of the kitchen, the teamwork is evident as servers swoop in and out at breakneck speeds depositing orders and picking up dishes.

"If you have dedicated your life to being a chef, this is the place to be," says Matt Merges, who was at Charlie Trotter's from 1989 to 1991 and returned

"The chefs here have their entire being focused on the plate. That's the difference between being very good and being great."—*Chef de cuisine Matt Merges*

in 1997 to become chef de cuisine. "This is not a place for *cooks*. It is a place for *chefs,* because this restaurant allows the chefs to put their souls on the plate." Merges, a New Jersey native who also sketches black-and-white food illustrations for Trotter's cookbooks, sees a direct relationship between the restaurant's philosophy and the quality of its food: "The chefs here have their entire being focused on the plate. That's the difference between being very good and being great."

The same spirit imbues the small staff in the front office as well. Like Merges and many other Trotter employees, controller Judi Carle enjoys wearing more than one hat. When she's not monitoring the cash flow, she serves as general editor of the restaurant's cookbooks. "We do things backwards here compared to the norm," she says, joking that the reason she was tapped to serve as editor is that she's the only person who can read Trotter's handwriting.

Charlie Trotter's original employee is Reginald Watkins, the morning sous-chef, who started as a dishwasher when the restaurant opened in 1987. Watkins, who grew up on the mean streets of a housing project on Chicago's South Side, arrives at 7 a.m. He spends the day preparing stocks for his sauces and inspecting the foodstuffs that have arrived from purveyors around the world. "My primary job is to see that chef Trotter gets his money's worth," he says.

Watkins has seen the restaurant change in numerous ways since its inception, but he says one thing remains the same: "Every plate has to pass through chef Trotter's hand before it goes to the customer. Everything had better be in place."

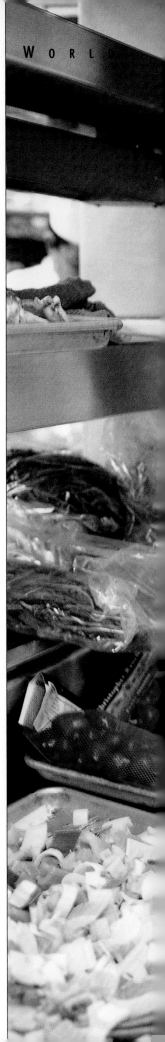

*Early morning
kitchen preparations
begin at 7 A.M.*

CHAPTER EIGHT

CUSTOMERS CONTENTED BEYOND THEIR WILDEST DREAMS

Prime goal of the waitstaff: Make the diner's experience a memorable one.

For Charlie Trotter's, there are no customers quite as special, yet quite as challenging, as Ray Harris and Steven Greystone. Harris, a Wall Street financier, has dined at Charlie Trotter's more than 250 times in the last five years. Greystone, vice president of a Boston software company, has eaten there nearly 150 times. Yet both say they've never had the same meal twice, confirming chef Trotter's claim that he never repeats a dish.

Both Harris and Greystone know food and wine. The globe-trotting executives have eaten in many of the great restaurants of the world, but the one they eagerly return to for an extraordinary dining experience is Charlie Trotter's. Surely, it is not the convenience. Both executives fly in from the East Coast to partake of Trotter's table.

Charlie Trotter's reputation draws the elite not only from the business community but from the ranks of rock stars, movie stars, politicians, athletes, authors, and even royalty. But out of respect for his guests' privacy, Trotter doesn't talk about famous visitors. Where some restaurants might call the gossip columnists to boast about their latest celebrity, he prefers to be discreet so that VIPs can feel

Lynn Trotter, center, with legendary diner George Rubenstein (left, who dined at the restaurant over 280 times) and prominent Chicago wine collector Stephen A. Kaplan.

comfortable in his restaurant. They can enjoy a quiet meal, because there are no red carpets, no special treatment.

Harris says he is never sure what to expect when he leaves the financial world behind and goes to Charlie Trotter's. "One night I went in after a tough day and mentioned that I wasn't feeling well," he recalls. "Charlie responded by serving me a menu of comfort food, including several bowls of soup. Other times, he's completely whimsical. He'll send a progression of dishes that are all made of corn or tomatoes. Sometimes, I think he just wants to see how long it will take me to figure out what he's up to."

Harris' first visit to Charlie Trotter's came late at night after a long day in the office. Although the kitchen was shutting down, Trotter fired up the lines and provided Harris with not just a meal but an experience that he still recalls enthusiastically. "Whether it was the atmosphere or the perfect combination of food and wine, I remember feeling as if this were my personal dining room," he says.

Harris was struck by the painstaking attention the chef and his staff paid to the smallest details, from the cuisine to the way each table was lovingly set. "I immediately recognized that Charlie Trotter has a passion for excellence," says Harris, who thinks it is well worth the expense to fly from New York City to enjoy the incomparable experience of eating at his favorite restaurant. "I knew right away that he was the best chef running the best table in Chicago. He rivals the best in California or New York. For that matter, he is operating at a level with the best in the world. I've never been there when it's been just a B+ evening."

Over the years, Trotter's employees have continued to impress Harris. "They work very long hours under exacting circumstances, and they are totally devoted," he says. "They are not people who simply punch a clock and deliv-

Chef Norman Van Aken, Chicago Legendary Chef Louie Szathmary,
Trotter, and Chef Emeril Lagasse.

Chef
Emeril Lagasse

er food to the table. They passionately describe the food and the wine."

Harris has observed how diligently the staff try to make dining at the restaurant a memorable experience, regardless of whether it is for a regular customer or someone making a once-in-a-lifetime visit. "The same level of attention is extended to anyone who walks through the door," he says. "The staff treat them as if they were royalty. The waiters patiently take the customers through the wine list, recommending food and wine matches."

Harris's wife, Shaun Butler, also a Wall Street executive, has joined her husband for dinner at Charlie Trotter's on several occasions. "I'm always impressed with the variety of the menu and the changing textures and taste of the food," she says. "There's always something new to try." Butler also likes the restaurant's understated atmosphere because it does not try to compete with the food on the plate or the wine in the glass.

Greystone, who flies from Boston to eat at Charlie Trotter's, says he keeps coming back because "it's such a joy to experience so many great dishes in the course of an evening, each one new, exciting, and beautifully presented."

For Greystone, Trotter's deserves its high rank in the gastronomical hierarchy. "I come here for dinner because there is no place like it in the United States," he says. "There are very few places in the world where you can eat as well. I am reminded of the great meals that I have had that were created by amazing chefs like Fredy Girardet in Switzerland or Tetsuya Wakuda in Australia, who epitomize the concept of cooking from the heart, not as a technician."

An international food and wine connoisseur, Greystone says he can tell a great restaurant even before he tastes the food "by watching what's going on. It's the attitude of the staff. It's the faces of the diners. It's the way

HARD TO PLEASE,
BUT NEVER IMPOSSIBLE

harlie Trotter's well-heeled clientele can be a demanding lot. They are particular about their food and wine, and they expect gracious service. Trotter and his staff try to accommodate even the most extraordinary customer requests.

One night, for example, a customer said that he just had to have a roast chicken, despite the fact that there was no chicken dish on any of the restaurant's three tasting menus. "Even though we are not a chicken restaurant, we would never tell a guest that," confides Trotter. He sent a chef out the back door and off to a local grocery store to find a chicken. The chef returned a short time later with a plump chicken and prepared a sumptuous feast. The guest consumed the roast chicken and went home happy. "He never knew what we had to do for him," says Trotter.

On the rare occasion when a guest claims to be dissatisfied with the dining experience, Trotter will invite the person back, even when the complaint seems dubious. A party of four men once complained that they didn't have enough to eat, despite a nearly three-hour, six-course meal that included several bottles of wine. Swallowing the expense, Trotter invited the foursome back for another six-course meal.

In an incident bordering on the surreal, Trotter even offered to foot the bill at his restaurant for a woman who complained about a meal she had eaten elsewhere. A local magazine had queried Trotter and others about their favorite cheap eats, and he had recommended an inexpensive restaurant on Chicago's North Shore that he sometimes visits. The woman wrote Trotter a sharp letter chastising him because she had visited the restaurant on the strength of his advice and been extremely disappointed with the food and the atmosphere. She said she couldn't understand how Trotter could have been so wrong about his choice of restaurants. To make amends, Trotter extended her an invitation, including round-trip cab fare, to come to his restaurant and enjoy a great meal on the house.

**Morell Mushroom, Sundried
Tomato "Tart" with Rabbit Loin
and Kidney.
(Charlie Trotter's Meat and Game)**

the place is moving. It's the whole ambience. You don't see busboys running around frantically at a great restaurant like Charlie Trotter's. Even when you walk into the rest room it's spotless."

Greystone maintains that you can also size up a restaurant by observing the little things, such as how fresh the flowers on the table are or how well the staff have cleaned the stemware. "The wine glasses at Trotter's are perfectly polished," he says. "I'd venture to say that 75 percent of all the wine glasses on restaurant tables today are improperly washed and have a detergent odor that ruins the wine."

The sommelier and the waitstaff at Trotter's are unusual in that they know how to open and decant a bottle of wine properly without disturbing the sediment, Greystone explains. "At Trotter's they've thought of everything, and they are doing it the right way. When I walk in the front door I know I can relax and let the staff take over. It's just such a special place. If I haven't been there in a month, I get kind of antsy."

He vividly recalls his first visit to Charlie Trotter's in 1990, when the restaurant was just beginning to serve degustation menus. "At that time, the desserts were à la carte. I was there with my brother, and we were debating which dessert to order, so we asked the waiter what he would recommend. He served that dessert, and then five minutes later he served us all the desserts that we couldn't make up our minds about. That's a perfect example of giving diners more than they expect."

Greystone remembers Trotter having a larger presence in the dining room in those early days. "On one of my first visits a man in a white jacket came out and began explaining the third course as he was serving it. I asked him to tell the chef how unbelievable the first two dishes were. He said that he would pass along the compliment, and then he bolted from the table. It wasn't until I was leaving that I saw the same guy saying good-bye to the guests and realized the man at my table had been Charlie Trotter."

*Regular guests know
they can count on service
that will exceed their
expectations.*

"There are very few places in the world where you can eat as well."—*Steven Greystone, customer*

Customers are amazed when they learn that Trotter has never served the same dish twice.

Based on his visits to Trotter's and other famous restaurants, Greystone has learned that a great restaurant experience is all about communicating. "It's a two-way street. The diner and the chef send subtle messages back and forth. If the diner gets psyched about the meal and begins to ask for something extra, the chef senses that and gets psyched himself. A chef is like an artist who wants his work appreciated."

Greystone marvels at Trotter's artistry. "I have never had the same dish twice," he says. "I might have some variations on a theme. I know I wouldn't be served a dish today that remotely resembles one I had seven years ago or even three years ago, because Charlie is now in a different phase. He is always pushing himself. He is always trying new things. He is always progressing as a chef."

Greystone, who traveled to New York City for the 1999 James Beard Foundation Restaurant Awards, where Trotter was named America's top chef, says Trotter's spontaneity is what sets him apart. "I've been in his restaurant many times and have seen him go off the page, if necessary. For example, if someone orders a wine that really doesn't go with the dish, he'll change the dish. There are very few restaurants that do the kind of things that he does in his kitchen."

But Charlie Trotter's is more than just food, says Greystone. "It's all about the Trotter philosophy: Do whatever it takes to get the job done. Nothing is impossible. They bend over backwards to accommodate you—to ensure that the diner is king. A lot of places claim to do that, but they can't quite pull it off."

Complete with an atrium, the foyer bar is a dramatic spot for entertaining.

CHARLIE TROTTER'S

CHAPTER NINE

WHEN A LANDMARK RESTAURANT THROWS A PARTY

Every night at Charlie Trotter's is designed to be memorable, but some are designed to be simply unforgettable. One evening in the winter of 1999, Trotter teamed up with the renowned French chef Marc Veyrat to create a menu featuring the best of both French and American cuisine. The master chefs alternated dishes during the eight-course meal. "Our guests were amazed by the food and delighted at being introduced to chef Veyrat," says Mark Signorio, the restaurant's special projects director. "We knew he would create a great event for them."

Trotter had long admired the flamboyant Veyrat, a Michelin three-star chef from the Auberge de l'Eridan on the shores of Lake Annecy in France's Savoy region. A botanist, Veyrat incorporates rare herbs from the alpine pastures of Savoy in his grand cuisine. He is known to mount 20-course dinners and prepare breakfasts that resemble royal feasts. Much like Trotter but unlike many French chefs, Veyrat eschews excessive butter and cream in his recipes.

On a pilgrimage to France in September 1998, Trotter invited Veyrat to visit Chicago and prepare some of his signature

"You learn after a while that it's not so much about competition, but rather, it is about how we can help each other out."—*Charlie Trotter*

It was a great day at the restaurant when master chef Paul Bocuse paid a visit.

dishes for the patrons of Charlie Trotter's. Veyrat resisted at first, recounting an unpleasant visit to New York City. Trotter assured him that the Midwest was different, so Veyrat came to Chicago, and in a big way. At Trotter's expense, Veyrat, his wife, his daughter (she is also his pastry chef), the sommelier, the maître d'hotel, and two chefs, flew business class to Chicago and stayed at the exclusive Whitehall Hotel for five days.

Veyrat and his entourage were accompanied by a 1,000-pound shipment of accoutrements, including Veyrat's favorite herbs, his specially designed glass plates, and autographed copies of his cookbook, *Fou de Saveurs* (Crazy about Taste). True to form, Veyrat used the plates that evening, wildly painting on sauces and overlaying them with delicate pieces of meat or fish.

Friends of the restaurant were invited to the $175-a-plate dinner (wine, tax, and tip extra), and every table in the 90-seat restaurant was reserved. Trotter, who normally focuses on activities in the kitchen, spent much of the evening in the dining room playing host and introducing Veyrat to everyone. If there were any language barriers, they quickly vanished. The guests were charmed by Veyrat, who speaks little English, and by his sommelier, Bruno Bozzer, and his maître d'hotel, Herve Audibert, both of whom speak it fluently. The waitstaff, inspired by the evening, sported colorful designer ties emblazoned with the image of Veyrat's distinctive chef's hat.

The following day, Trotter invited 22 top chefs from Chicago and nearby cities for a five-hour chef's luncheon in the restaurant's studio kitchen. Trotter played second banana, assisting Veyrat as he displayed his culinary virtuosity for the Americans, most of whom were meeting him for the first time. Trotter prides himself on the relationship he has with other Chicago chefs. "You learn after a while that it's not so much about competition as about how we can help each other out,"

For one of Trotter's more memorable occasions, Chef Marc Veyrat flew in from France with several hundred pounds of accoutrements.

Chef Marc Veyrat, Lynn Trotter, and Veyrat's wife Annick.

he says. "We're all proud of the fact that we're making Chicago a great dining destination. It's a win-win situation for everyone."

His instinct for bringing people together in a good cause is responsible for many of the events at the restaurant. Evenings like the one with Veyrat are done with cultural and culinary goals in mind. Others are usually intended to raise funds for one of the many charities that Trotter supports.

In the spring of 1999, Trotter filled the restaurant on a Sunday night with guests who paid $125 a plate to honor the memory of Patrick Clark. Clark, considered the nation's preeminent African-American chef at the time of his death, had been the executive chef at New York's Tavern on the Green. He was awaiting a heart transplant when he died at age 42, leaving his wife, Lynette, and their five young children. His medical expenses were astronomical, and he had no health insurance.

In addition to the proceeds from the dinner, funds to help the family were raised by selling copies of *Cooking with Patrick Clark: A Tribute to the Man and His Cuisine,* the cookbook that Trotter had helped Clark complete before he died (*see* Chapter 11).

The menu that night reflected Clark's distinctive touch. Among the dishes were pan-roasted sea bass with lump crab, sweet peas, and fava beans; rabbit loin with leeks and wild mushrooms; and Merlot-braised short ribs with horseradish mashed potatoes. The wines were all produced in American vineyards. Desserts included lemon pudding cake and pecan banana tart.

Lynette Clark attended the dinner, and the menu included the following tribute to her husband: "Patrick Clark was one of the first celebrity chefs in America, a pioneer in the regional cuisine movement, and a role model for other African-Americans interested in the culinary arts. But Clark was much more than that. He was not just a great chef, he

Watching the monitor overhead, guests can see their meal being prepared in the main kitchen.

Photograph, Jesse Walker

COURTING CLIENTS IN THE KITCHEN

One of the best places to do business in Chicago seems to be the small kitchen that serves as a studio for Charlie Trotter's TV show. Three or four nights a week, executives from such industries as financial services, publishing, and electronics reserve the handsomely appointed kitchen and its adjoining dining room to entertain clients, introduce a new product, or celebrate the closing of a big deal.

The studio kitchen has become especially popular with pharmaceutical companies, which invite their doctor clients to the restaurant to sell them on their latest products. One doctor, who had resisted every one of a pharmaceutical rep's previous overtures, relented when he heard the dinner was going to be at Trotter's.

A chef, two waiters, and a sommelier are assigned to the studio kitchen, and several of the dishes are prepared right there. Two overhead TV monitors in the 20-seat dining room allow guests to watch their other dishes being prepared in the main kitchen. With so many gastronomic temptations on the plate in front of them and on the screen above them, clients may not focus entirely on business, but the studio kitchen is still much in demand.

Trotter prides himself on the relationship he has with other Chicago chefs.

was a culinary leader, a gentleman, and most importantly a devoted father and husband. It was easy to be inspired by his talent, his vision, his charisma. His humor and his generosity knew no bounds."

That same evening, more than 40 other restaurants throughout the country sponsored Patrick Clark dinners featuring his favorite recipes. As at Trotter's, diners bought copies of Clark's cookbook and offered support to the family.

Waiters at Trotters helped sell copies of the book throughout the evening, and when diners had finished their meals, their waiters led them on a tour of the restaurant's kitchens and wine cellars. For most, the evening included a chat with Trotter, who talked about his friendship with Clark and the many conversations they had about writing a cookbook. Nearly everyone left the restaurant with a copy of *Cooking with Patrick Clark*.

Perhaps the grandest night of all was August 17, 1997, when Charlie Trotter's celebrated its tenth anniversary. The formally attired guests received engraved invitations and paid $1,000 a plate to benefit one of Charlie Trotter's favorite charities, the Mercy Home for Boys and Girls on Chicago's West Side. Eight youngsters from the home were on hand to greet the guests at the door. It was the first time the restaurant had put on a $1,000-a-plate charity dinner.

Two luminaries from the European food and wine scene flew in for the occasion. One was Roger Verge, the legendary chef from Moulin de Mougins near Cannes; the other was Angelo Gaya, a famous Italian wine producer. The restaurant, from the wine cellar to the kitchen to the dining rooms, was festooned with flowers. A tent was set up on the rear deck where everyone enjoyed a reception in the evening air. After dinner was served, Trotter brought Verge and Gaya to each dining room to introduce his special guests to the diners.

The anniversary dinner was successful, Trotter says, because it was not just a fundraiser. The appearance of Verge and Gaya gave it a cultural and culinary dimension. The highlight of the evening, nevertheless, was the announcement that the occasion netted $75,000 for the Mercy Home.

The following day, Verge and Gaya were feted at a chef's luncheon. Twenty young Chicago-area chefs joined the guests of honor in the studio kitchen. It was an opportunity for the younger chefs to meet and be inspired by two legends in the world of food and wine.

Trotter with Steve Greystone, who has dined at the restaurant on more than 150 occasions.

*Critics give Trotter high marks
for a restless culinary imagination. Above, his Amberjack with
Periwinkle Vinaigrette, Wild Watercress, and Shallot Blossom.*
(Charlie Trotter's Seafood)

CHAPTER TEN

RECOGNITION FOR A NEW CULINARY LEADER

*C*harlie Trotter's harshest critic is himself. The food writers and restaurant critics are no match for his searing self-criticism, which may explain why he doesn't take the reviews too seriously, regardless of whether they are good or bad.

Despite a dismissive attitude toward the critics, Trotter has fared well at their hands over the years. In fact, he acknowledges that the restaurant was fortunate to have positive reviews from newspaper and magazine food critics early in the game. Example: After it opened in August 1987, John Mariani of *Esquire* hailed Trotter's as one of America's best new restaurants.

Just a month after the opening, the *Chicago Tribune* reported that "Charlie Trotter's is more than just another pretty restaurant. The restaurant takes its name from its 28-year-old chef/owner, whose attention to culinary detail equals the care that went into the decor. Trotter's style represents the best of the 'new American cooking.' He emphasizes simple preparations based on the French tradition, borrows ideas from various other cultures, and keeps his dishes light, usually flavored with the even-handed use of fresh herbs."

By the time the restaurant hit its stride in December 1990, *Crain's Chicago Business* wrote that "Charlie Trotter's is perfect for entertaining people who care passionately about food. Everything about the two-story townhouse restaurant contributes to the enjoyment of the meal: the unexpected, yet elegant decor, the extremely knowledgeable staff, the broad wine list. . . . The upstairs dining room (a smoking section, alas) and recently added private room feel airy compared with the slightly cramped down-

*Above, the kitchen refurbished. From the start, Trotter caught the interest
of writers intrigued by the new American cooking (opposite).*

stairs, but even that is well-lighted, so you can see what you're eating.   And there's so much to see. Each dish emerges from chef Trotter's kitchen a work of art—exuberant yet refined; often experimental, always elaborate."

In 1994, *Restaurant Business* observed that "Charlie Trotter's is in a quiet private dwelling, with menus in degustation rather than an à la carte format. Dishes change from day to day. Guests can choose a smaller five-course meal, or from two eight-course options, one vegetarian, one omnivorous. Each night, Trotter offers a ten-part, spontaneously created menu. These creative outbursts are the main event, really, attracting as many as 70 percent of diners. For Trotter, each dish is a piece on the chessboard that must be considered in relation to other dishes on the menu. They're designed to be eaten completely without leaving diners to stumble off uncomfortably full. In addition, each move in the kitchen implies a new wine possibility. Though the combinations are endlessly intricate, servers operate strictly from memory."

In 1995, Trotter invited *Esquire's* Mariani to the restaurant, vowing that he would enjoy the greatest meal of his life. Mariani's review said, in part: "Rankled by my comments that sometimes his food was too showy and too contrived and that he spent too much time on the celebrity chefs' circuit, Trotter wanted to prove what so many others have contended: that he is the finest American-born chef of his generation and certainly one of the most

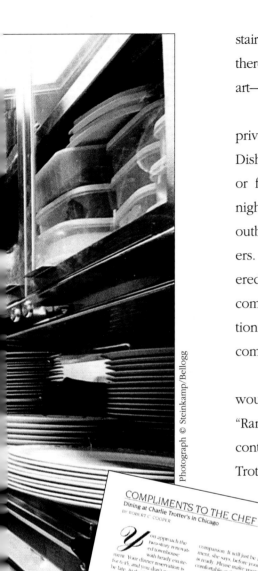

influential. . . . Okay, was it the greatest meal of my life? No. Was it a great meal? Yes. Despite his flourish of serving six different canapés as part of the first course and six different desserts as the last, the meal was remarkably light and impeccably matched."

Mariani praised Trotter's service staff as among the best he had encountered, lauded the depth of the wine list, and declared all the restaurant's amenities as first-class. Concluding, he asked rhetorically, "Is Trotter the greatest American chef working today? Not yet, though he may be the hardest-working and most driven. Delacroix once said of young painters, 'Talent does whatever it wants to do, genius only what it can do.' Trotter, who is only thirty-five, is clearly doing everything he can with his formidable gifts. He is a work in progress that no lover of the best food can afford to miss."

That same year, Molly O'Neill of *The New York Times* wrote, "I know of no other chef like Charlie Trotter. The complexity of his recipes pushes the outer limits of culinary sanity. But more often than not, they are ingenious, [and they are] invariably beautiful. Trotter believes in serving a succession of small, ornate dishes (constructions really), each no more than a taste, one more complex than the next. He'll stuff rabbit rilette, for example, into tiny columns of phyllo dough. Then he'll fry them, cut them like Vietnamese spring rolls and mount them like tiny rock pilings in a sea of oranges, black olives, and reduced rabbit broth. His lasagna of braised turnips and rabbit is built like a shingled pagoda, floating on a sauce of sweet peas."

Charlie Trotter's was the center of attention in 1997, the year it marked its tenth anniversary. "This could be Charlie Trotter's big year," wrote the *Atlanta Constitution*. "Just as his temple of haute cuisine celebrates its tenth anniversary, he also has a James Beard nomination for best American chef tucked under his apron. . . . Dropping by recently to see what the fuss is all about, we found the answer not so much in the elegant trappings of the clubby-feeling townhouse (a discreet brass plaque instead of a sign; Biedermeier furniture in the lobby; a swagged and bro-caded main room; servers in designer suits) as in the fan-tastical seven-course degustation menu. What joy to dis-cover nuggets of lobster and smoked salmon hidden under a disc of yellowfin tuna, the whole thing flecked with caviar and surrounded with a strand of tiny oysters. And that was just the first plate."

In a September 1997 cover story for *Chicago* magazine, Jonathan Black wrote, "But is this restaurant for you? Where does Charlie Trotter's figure in your meal plan? If you're one

Trotter consistently confounds the experts by transforming everyday ingredients into an exotic feast.

122

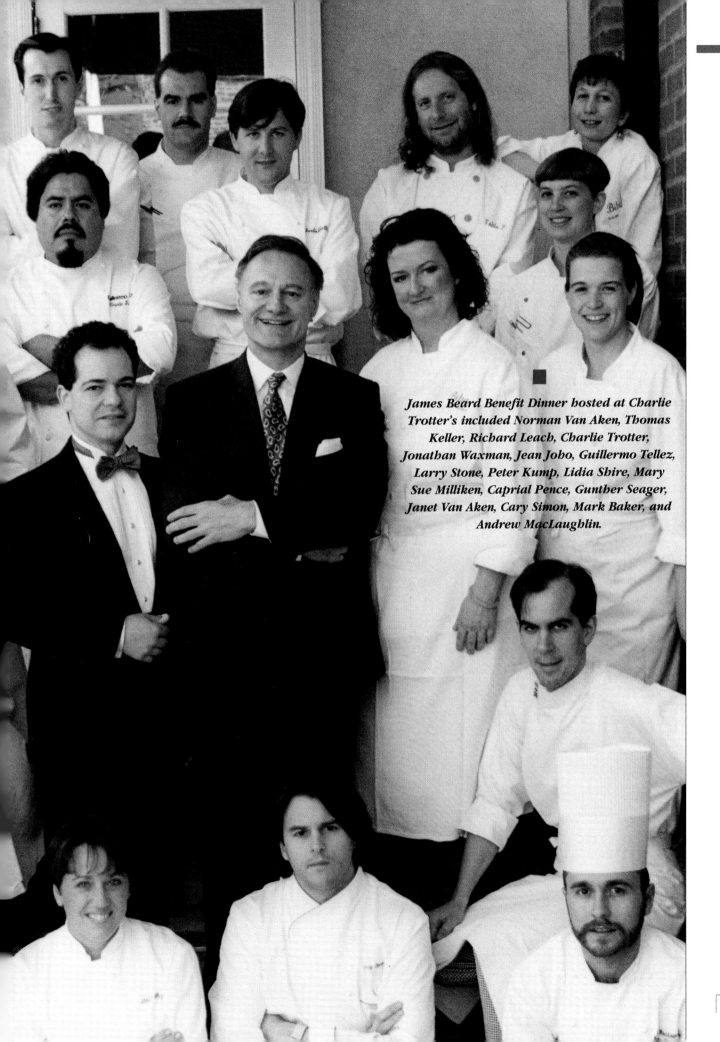

James Beard Benefit Dinner hosted at Charlie Trotter's included Norman Van Aken, Thomas Keller, Richard Leach, Charlie Trotter, Jonathan Waxman, Jean Joho, Guillermo Tellez, Larry Stone, Peter Kump, Lidia Shire, Mary Sue Milliken, Caprial Pence, Gunther Seager, Janet Van Aken, Cary Simon, Mark Baker, and Andrew MacLaughlin.

"The Tasting Menu Is Meant to Dazzle"

Newsweek could not have picked a better time for a story about Charlie Trotter as part of a trend piece on multicourse restaurant meals. The article, which ran under the headline, "Now, It's Designer Meals," ran on April 26, 1999, and the following week, Trotter, a master of the tasting menu, received the Outstanding Chef Award from the James Beard Foundation.

Wrote *Newsweek*: "The brilliant chef Charlie Trotter, in creating the Chicago restaurant that bears his name, decided to proceed by asking himself each day, 'What do I want to eat tonight?' and then trusting that the answer will appeal to his customers. He does four tasting menus each night, including a vegetarian version and one for people who want to drink only red wines. An even more stupendously delectable 12-course, three-hour extravaganza is served only at a single table inside the kitchen, priced at $150 per person.

"Running a kitchen this way is incomparably more complex than keeping up with even a very large a la carte menu. Each night's menus must be created afresh, and even created on the fly. You never know when someone's going to show up with a salsify allergy, or who had the roasted saddle of Scottish hare with red-wine boudin emulsion for lunch, requiring a sudden substitution. The tasting menu is meant to dazzle. Trotter claims he has had one customer return 265 times and has never served him the same meal twice."

of those diners with a favorite dish, forget it. You swooned over last month's halibut with turnip infusion? Put it out of your mind. The halibut is history. The very idea of a signature dish is an insult to Charlie. Might as well ask Leonardo to draw another *Mona Lisa*. In other words, don't make the trek to Armitage if you think in categories. And don't come around if your idea of haute cuisine is a lump of perfectly cooked protein in a fabulous deglazed sauce. That centerpiece of French haute cuisine leaves Charlie yawning. Save your money, in fact, if you're looking for sauces at all.

"Charlie is into broths. Very light, wispy vegetable infusions. True, you might find a nice butter-rich sauce over a cube of pompano. But butter and cream are not exactly staples here. Nor, to be candid, are meats. It's not that Charlie is a health nut. No, there is simply not enough Charlie can do to a piece of meat. But vegetables—ah . . . vegetables are another matter. And, oh, yes, skip the entire experience if you like normal portions. Even the desserts are tiny little things. And speaking of desserts, don't come around expecting a wheeled cheese cart laden with biscuits, grapes, and smelly stuff from France."

Trotter's impressive wine selection has won accolades over the years, and in that anniversary year it received its usual praise from *Wine Spectator*: "Sommelier Joseph Spellman organizes the cellar, a *Wine Spectator* Grand Award winner since 1993, and can make inspired suggestions. The food repays vinous exploration, too. Squab with morels and a delicate curry emulsion complemented a glass of Chavy Puligny-Montrachet 1994 ($16). A scallop with foie gras

Trotter's ability to come up with new tasting menus night after night has always impressed food writers.

and red wine essence set off a glass of Jean-Michel Gaunoux Pommard 1993 ($16). Red wine with scallops, white with rare squab. Perfectly natural here."

Not content to stop there, *Wine Spectator* continued: "The wine list offers plenty to plunder, including such fascinating offbeat selections as a sparkling wine from Mas de Daumus Gassac or a dozen hot new wines from Australia. No weak choices clog the list, which is strong in areas that work with the food: Alsatian, German, Rhone in red and white, plus extraordinary red and white Burgundy in good vintages. Red Bordeaux shows some depth (17 vintages of Mouton-Rothschild back to '28). California reds lack depth, but they hit many of the hottest names in recent vintages."

The 1999 edition of the prestigious Relais & Châteaux directory said Charlie Trotter, "one of the brightest stars of American gastronomy, is renowned for his innovative cuisine, inspired by the culinary cultures from around the world. Gourmets will adore his organic lamb rack with braised cabbage, white bean puree, brussels sprouts, and meat juice and his Alaskan halibut with fiddlehead ferns, asparagus and cardamom infused carrot juice. The award-wining cellar, stocked with 1,100 vintages, is superb."

In March 1999 *Travel & Leisure* magazine held forth on Trotter's: "If you own an NFL franchise, Gulfstream IV jet, or a case of '82 Petrus, Charlie Trotter's may well be your favorite restaurant in the world. A coolly handsome dining room in a Lincoln Park townhouse, Charlie Trotter's is famous for its multicourse tasting menus, as exquisitely choreographed as a Jerome Robbins entr'acte. The wine list is dictionary-size, but most people trust the sommelier's choices for wine by the glass. And a meal here ...

FINE DINING
HALL OF FAME
Charlie Trotter's

Charlie Trotter's excites Chicagoans with modern approach to classical food

By Carolyn Walkup

Charlie Trotter's has redefined French-influenced fine dining in Chicago. "We're not so pretentious or flamboyantly formal, but every bit as detailed, efficient and refined," says the intense, young Trotter, who is largely self-taught. "How we present things and put them together is different, but the combinations of ingredients are classic."

The drive and energy that goes on behind the scenes also is integral to Trotter's success. Trotter credits the "sincere, conscientious, generous, perfectionist-oriented" attitudes of the people who work at the restaurant with making Trotter's unique.

His first exposure to restaurant work occurred more than eight years ago when he worked for Gordon Sinclair, another Hall of Fame winner. Later he worked briefly in a few well-known San Francisco restaurants, studied for six months at the California Culinary Academy and spent six months in France on a personal culinary education odyssey.

Upon his return home, he catered dinners for Chicago's social and political leaders in their homes. Many of his catering customers would become his first restaurant guests only a year later.

Since opening his restaurant less than four years ago, Trotter has taken local foodies by storm with his ever-changing, seasonal menus. Although menu descriptions are lengthy, the look and taste of the final result always surprises and even enchants.

"All the dishes are based on classical combinations of things. How we present things and put them together is different. We never went out in left field," Trotter explains.

Dedicated to using organic or naturally raised products as much as possible, Trotter also emphasizes vegetables more than most fine-dining operators do. A nine-course vegetable menu degustation now accounts for about 23 percent of dinner orders.

Theme degustations are one of

Charlie Trotter, chef and co-owner of Charlie Trotter's restaurant in Chicago.

Charlie Trotter's
816 W. Armitage Ave.
Chicago, Ill. 60614
(312) 248-6228

Owners: Charlie and Robert Trotter.
Chef: Charlie Trotter.
Year opened: 1987.
Cuisine: French-influenced American.
Seats: 70.
Check average: $90 dinner.

15

Fine Dining Hall of Fame, May 6, 1991

Reviewers have praised Trotter for an approach to cooking that allows innovation to flourish in a classical tradition.

"The very idea of a signature dish is an insult to Charlie. Might as well ask Leonardo to draw another *Mona Lisa.*" — *Jonathan Black,* Chicago *magazine*

Roger Verge (center) with Guillermo Tellez, Daniel Boulud, Andrew MacLaughlin, Charlie Trotter, Robert Morris, and Larry Stone.

may cost a cool hundred clams, tax, tip, wine, and coffee not included. Trotter's virtuosity is unequaled in this part of the country."

After it was announced that Trotter had been honored with the Outstanding Chef Award by the James Beard Foundation in May 1999, the *Chicago Sun-Times* published a full-page feature article that said, in part: "In the fine dining world, Trotter, 39, has been likened to Michael Jordan—a comparison he doesn't shy from—and has been called one of Chicago's meanest people for his unrelenting perfectionism and drive. His creations, offered each night in degustation menus, are not mere dishes, but things of beauty, their elements swirled, stacked, sculpted, and polished into small, precious jewels. The signature quality of 'Trotter's food' is the use of fresh ingredients, drawn as often as possible from regional sources, part of a network of scores of suppliers. The menu offers descriptions of such complexity that they are often hard to fathom until the dish arrives at the table."

Despite the raves, *Crain's Chicago Business* wrote a front-page story in April 1999 speculating that the entrepreneurial Trotter is spreading himself too thin with all his ventures. The article, headlined "Is Charlie Trotter Running too Fast?," mentioned Trotter's TV series, his celebrity-chef deal with United Airlines, and his plans to launch a restaurant in 2001 at the American Center for Wine and Food in California's Napa Valley.

Those close to Trotter counter that, despite his entrepreneurial ventures, he is maintaining the right balance. Ironically, his TV show may have created the impression that Trotter is suddenly everywhere, but the fact is that the shows are taped right in the restaurant's studio kitchen.

For his part, Trotter is not one to hang on every word from the critics. "Their reviews have no bearing on what we do here," he says. "I don't think the critics can begin to understand all the subtleties of this business; otherwise, they'd be doing it themselves. I can only answer to myself and the feedback of my customers."

*On hand for the American Cancer Society's VinAffair: Art of the Earth dinner in 1999 were Daniel Boulud,
Restaurant Daniel, New York City; Mark Baker, Seasons at the Four Seasons, Chicago; Charlie Trotter;
Jeffrey Steingarten, food critic, Vogue; Ferran Adria, El Bulli, Barcelona; Gordon Ramsay of Gordon Ramsay,
London; Tetsuya Wakuda, Tetsuya's, Sydney; and Norman Van Aken, Norman's, Miami.*

CHAPTER ELEVEN

MAKING AN IMPACT ON THE CITY AND BEYOND

Besides being a creative chef and a relentless taskmaster, Charlie Trotter is a hard-driving capitalist with the soft touch of a philanthropist. Although the restaurant is a small business, Trotter's entrepreneurial ventures enable him to play a philanthropic role in Chicago, the nation, and the culinary community at large.

In his hometown of Chicago, his cooking demonstrations have benefited such organizations as the Chicago Fund on Aging and Disability, Literacy Chicago, the Make-A-Wish Foundation, the March of Dimes, the American Cancer Society, and Providence St. Mel, an inner-city Catholic high school.

In a typical scenario, Trotter invites 30 guests to his studio kitchen on a Saturday afternoon. He charges $100 a head for people to witness his wizardry, pepper him with questions, and sample his culinary handiwork. The 90-minute demonstration invariably leaves them oohing and aahing with delight, and the $3,000 goes to the sponsoring organization.

Trotter has also helped raise money for leading cultural institutions in the city, such as the Lyric Opera, the Goodman Theatre, and the Ravinia Festival Music Center. "We orchestrated the American Cancer Society's VinAffair wine auction and dinner, which helped them raise more than $800,000," he says. "We're not doing this for public relations. That's not the point. It's to do something that makes a difference."

Trotter also raises money by suggesting that visiting chefs who come to learn his techniques donate $1,000 to a favorite Trotter charity for every week they spend in his kitchen.

The restaurant's most successful form of fund-raising, however, is its Guest Chef for a Day program. For example, the Maag Toy Foundation, which raises money to buy toys for underprivileged children in Chicago, put a Guest Chef certificate on the block at its annual golf outing and auction. People sometimes bid more than $3,000 for the chance to don a toque and spend an evening working in one of America's most famous kitchens. Trotter gives away about 20 of the certificates to local charities every month.

Advancing the cause of good cuisine is another of Trotter's concerns. Locally, he serves as a member of Chicago's Kennedy-King College Culinary Advisory Board. His main contribution on the national culinary scene is as a trustee of the James Beard Foundation. At the James Beard House in New York City, he has helped raise money by putting on cooking demonstrations.

His influence in the culinary community was most evident in April 1999 when more than 40 leading restaurants around the country sponsored special dinners in memory of Patrick Clark, the renowned African-American chef who had died a year before. Trotter, a close friend of Clark's, organized the national event to mark the release of Clark's cookbook, *Cooking with Patrick Clark: A Tribute to the Man and His Cuisine.* Royalties from the $35 book were assigned to the Patrick Clark Family Trust, a nonprofit fund created to assist in the education and support of Clark's five young children.

People sometimes bid more than $3,000 for the chance to don a toque and spend an evening working in Trotter's kitchen.

Activity during a charitable event can be as intense as on a Saturday evening.

Tough Love in the Pastry Department

In addition to his charitable contributions and fund-raising efforts, Charlie Trotter makes it a point to reach out to individuals. At the restaurant's tenth anniversary dinner, which raised $75,000 for the Mercy Home for Boys and Girls, he saw an opportunity to help again when he heard the story of Aaron Lindgren.

Lindgren, a young man who had once lived at the home, had impressed the director, the Rev. James Close. Thanks to Close, he had attended cooking school at Kendall College in suburban Evanston and gone on to a series of jobs in bakeries in the Chicago area and Colorado. On learning that Lindgren needed a chance to hone his skills, Trotter offered to put him to work in the restaurant's pastry department, where he would be exposed to a team of top chefs.

It was not the first time Trotter has taken a chance by helping a youngster. He also mentored Siron Young, who grew up amid the violence of Chicago's Cabrini-Green housing project. When Trotter takes a kid under his wing, he expects the young person to work as hard as anyone else in his bustling kitchen, and both Lindgren and Young learned hard lessons under his exacting gaze (Lindgren likened the experience to being in the military). Both young men "graduated" from Trotter's and went on to work in other Chicago restaurants.

Some relationships are more permanent. When Trotter was starting out in 1987, he hired a young man from the projects named Reginald Watkins as a dish-washer. Watkins, who has been with the restaurant longer than any other employee, is now the morning sous-chef. Says he, "The chef and I have shared our blood, sweat, and tears in here since day one."

Trotter and his staff had been instrumental in producing the book. "Patrick was always curious about how to publish a cookbook," recalls Trotter, who advised Clark to save his recipes and notes assiduously for that purpose. But as he grew ill with a rare blood disorder, it was impossible for Clark to continue writing.

That's when Trotter stepped in. He asked fellow chefs around the country to contribute some of their recipes that could be interspersed with Clark's. They were also asked to contribute a personal recollection about Clark for the book. Chefs, notorious for their foot-dragging on everything but preparing food, responded quickly. The finished product, handsomely designed and exquisitely illustrated, combined a trove of Clark's hand-scrawled recipes with the contributions of the other chefs.

"Charlie didn't have to do that," says Ray Harris, the Wall Street executive who is Trotter's most frequent diner. "But he did, and I think that's why he commands the respect of the industry."

One important aspect of community relations begins right at the curb, says Trotter, who has made a point of having the restaurant blend in with the tasteful surroundings of his Lincoln Park neighborhood. The former townhouse is part of an eclectic urban streetscape on West Armitage Avenue that includes expensive

**Slow-Roasted Salmon with
Red Wine Risotto, Wild Thyme,
and Tiny White Asparagus.**

*Rice Beans and Matsutake Mushrooms
wrapped in Red Swiss Chard with
Garlic-Mushroom Broth and Tarragon.*
(Charlie Trotter's Vegetables)

TURNING SECOND-GRADERS INTO GOURMETS

For Trotter's son, Dylan, and his classmates, the bustling restaurant was just the place to learn about manners.

One of Charlie Trotter's favorite occasions was the time he played host to 65 second-graders from his son Dylan's school. The students, accompanied by their teachers and the school principal, came attired in blue blazers for the boys and dresses for the girls. They were exceptionally well behaved, and with good reason. Prior to the luncheon, Trotter had met with them on three Wednesdays to discuss the theme for the event: "Manners, Civility, and Kindness."

As part of the project, the children created decorations, wrote invitations, and worked with Trotter developing several menu options, which they then voted on. The winning dessert was apple pie with ice cream. Although desserts are usually more exotic at Charlie Trotter's, the chef was happy to accommodate the request and the kids went home happy. "Events like that are a great satisfaction," says Trotter. "Sometimes I can't believe I get to do this."

"We're not doing this for public relations. It's to do something that makes a difference."—*Charlie Trotter*

boutiques, banks, a bakery, an optical shop, and a Baptist church.

A vine of concord grapes crawls up the restaurant's front wall, and pleasant aromas are given off by pots of mint and a crate of apples arranged on the steps. The only indication that this is a restaurant is a discreet brass plaque engraved with the words, "Charlie Trotter's." Says the boss, "It's all about subtlety. I hate big signage and gaudiness."

Overall, however, Trotter's plans for the restaurant's contribution to the community are anything but modest. As his enterprise grows, he plans to remain active in the culinary world and to continue supporting numerous charities and cultural organizations. "We want to make sure," he says, "that we're doing something that makes a difference in a lot of places."

■

James Beard Benefit Dinner with (from left) Charlie Trotter, Susie Crofton, Gordon Sinclair, Norman Van Aken, Celeste Zecola, and Carrie Nahabedian.

Guests at the Kitchen Table with Charlie.

It takes a versatile chef to combine pumpkin soup, pheasant, and ginger.

CHARLIE TROTTER'S

CHAPTER TWELVE

RECIPES FROM CHARLIE TROTTER'S

Pumpkin Soup with Pheasant Breast and Fried Ginger

(From *The Kitchen Sessions with Charlie Trotter*)

Serves 4

1 small pumpkin (about 1 1/2 pounds), halved and seeded

Salt and pepper

3 tablespoons olive oil

12 sprigs thyme

1/4 cup Preserved Ginger (*see* recipe page 142)

2 cups Chicken Stock (*see* recipe page 143)

3 tablespoons butter

1/2 cup julienned fresh ginger

1/2 cup plus 1 tablespoon canola oil

2 pheasant breasts, skin on

1/4 cup dried cranberries, chopped and rehydrated

1/4 cup pepitos (green pumpkin seeds)

4 teaspoons pumpkin seed oil

To prepare the pumpkin:

Rub the pumpkin with the olive oil and season with salt and pepper. Place the pumpkin halves upside down on a sheet pan and place 8 of the thyme sprigs under the pumpkins. Add 1/4 inch of water and roast at 350 F for 45 to 60 minutes, or until the pumpkins are tender.

To prepare the soup:

Puree the Preserved Ginger, its syrup, the Chicken Stock, and the pulp from the cooked pumpkin until smooth, and season to taste with salt and pepper. Cook the mixture over medium heat for 5 minutes, or until warm. Whisk in the butter and season to taste with salt and pepper.

To prepare the ginger:

Place the julienned ginger and 1/2 cup of room-temperature canola oil in a small saucepan. Warm the oil over medium heat and cook for 8 to 10 minutes, or until golden brown and crispy. Drain on paper towels.

To prepare the pheasant:

Season the pheasant with salt and pepper. Add the remaining 1 tablespoon canola oil to a hot sauté pan over medium heat. Add the pheasant and cook for 3 to 5 minutes on each side, or until just cooked. Let stand for 3 minutes and then thinly slice. Season to taste with salt and pepper.

Assembly:

Ladle the soup into 4 shallow bowls. Arrange the pheasant slices in the center, and sprinkle the dried cranberries, pepitos, fried ginger, and the remaining thyme leaves around the bowl. Top with freshly ground black pepper and drizzle the pumpkin seed oil around the edge.

Preserved Ginger

Yield: about 3/4 cup

1 cup finely julienned ginger

1 1/2 cups Simple Syrup (*see* note below)

Blanch the ginger in simmering water for 3 minutes. Strain and repeat the process 2 more times. Simmer the ginger in the Simple Syrup for 30 minutes. Remove from the heat and cool in the syrup. Refrigerate in the syrup until needed.

Note: To prepare Simple Syrup, bring 2 cups water and 2 cups sugar to a boil, remove the pan from the heat and let cool. The syrup may be kept for up to 1 month in the refrigerator.

Chicken Stock

Yield: 2 quarts

6 pounds chicken bones

3 cups chopped onions

2 cups chopped carrots

2 cups chopped celery

1 cup chopped leeks

1 tablespoon white peppercorns

1 bay leaf

Place all of the ingredients in a large stockpot and cover three-quarters of the way with cold water. Bring to a boil, reduce the heat to low, and slowly simmer, uncovered, for 4 hours, skimming every 30 minutes to remove impurities that rise to the surface. Strain, discard the solids, and cook over medium heat for 30 to 45 minutes, or until reduced to 2 quarts. Store in the refrigerator for up to 2 days or freeze for up to 2 months.

Seared Tuna with Fennel Broth, Herbed Spaetzle, and Sun-Dried Tomatoes

(From *Charlie Trotter's Seafood*)

Serves 4

1 egg, beaten

2 tablespoons chopped parsley

1 cup flour

1/2 cup milk

Salt and pepper

6 cups fennel juice (about 10 bulbs)

2 cups julienned fennel

3 tablespoons canola oil

12 ounces tuna loin

1/4 cup sun-dried tomatoes, julienned

4 teaspoons olive oil

4 teaspoons coarsely chopped
   fennel tops

To prepare the spaetzle:

Combine the egg, parsley, and flour. Add enough milk to make a somewhat stiff batter. Cover and refrigerate for 1 hour. Using a pastry bag or spaetzle maker, drop 1/4 teaspoonfuls of batter into simmering, lightly salted water. Cook for 1 minute, or until the spaetzle floats. Drain the spaetzle and season to taste with salt and pepper. (Toss the spaetzle with a little olive oil if you are not using it immediately.)

To prepare the broth:

Bring the fennel juice to a simmer and cook for 5 minutes. Strain the juice through a fine-mesh sieve lined with cheesecloth or a coffee filter and season to taste with salt and pepper.

As in any great art, finishing touches count for a lot.

To prepare the fennel:

Sauté the julienned fennel in 1 tablespoon of the canola oil for 5 minutes, or until golden brown. Season with salt and pepper.

To prepare the tuna:

Season the tuna with salt and pepper and place in a very hot sauté pan with the remaining 2 tablespoons of canola oil. Quickly sear the tuna on each side and remove from the pan, leaving the tuna rare inside. Slice the tuna into 20 thin slices and season to taste with salt and pepper.

Assembly:

Place some of the sun-dried tomatoes, julienned fennel, and spaetzle in the center of each bowl. Arrange 5 of the tuna slices over the spaetzle and ladle in some of the fennel broth. Drizzle the olive oil around each bowl and sprinkle with the fennel tops. Top with freshly ground pepper.

Chilled Pork Salad with Walnuts, Cantaloupe, Jicama, and Cumin Vinaigrette

(From *The Kitchen Sessions with Charlie Trotter*)

Serves 4

4 teaspoons cumin seeds, toasted and coarsely ground	2 tablespoons canola oil
4 1/2 tablespoons raspberry vinegar	1 red onion, julienned
1/4 cup olive oil	1 tablespoon butter
1/3 cup walnut oil	4 cups watercress, stemmed
Salt and pepper	2 cups julienned cantaloupe
2 thick-cut boneless pork chops (or pork loin)	1/2 cup walnuts, toasted and chopped
	1 cup peeled and julienned jicama

To prepare the vinaigrette:

Place the cumin and raspberry vinegar in a small bowl and slowly whisk in the olive oil and walnut oil. Season to taste with salt and pepper.

To prepare the pork:

Season the pork with salt and pepper. Place the canola oil in a hot sauté pan over high heat and sear the pork for 2 to 3 minutes on each side, or until golden brown. Reduce the heat to medium, cover, and cook for 5 to 7 minutes, or until the pork has an internal temperature of 150 F. Reserve any pan juices and refrigerate the meat for 1 hour, or until completely chilled. Thinly slice the pork and season to taste with salt and pepper.

To prepare the onion:

Cook the onion in the butter over medium-high heat for 5 minutes, or until golden and caramelized. Season to taste with salt and pepper.

To prepare the salad:

Toss together the watercress, onion, cantaloupe, walnuts, jicama, and three-quarters of the vinaigrette. Season to taste with salt and pepper.

Assembly:

Place some of the salad in the center of each plate and top with a few of the pork slices. Spoon the remaining vinaigrette and pan juices over the pork and around the plates. Top with freshly ground pepper.

Sea Scallops with Blended Chicken Liver Sauce and Braised Collard Greens

(From *The Kitchen Sessions with Charlie Trotter*)

Serves 4

1/4 cup chopped uncooked bacon	4 cups chopped collard greens
1 cup chopped onions	1/2 teaspoon sugar
4 chicken livers	1 tablespoon balsamic vinegar
Salt and pepper	8 sea scallops
2 tablespoons butter	2 tablespoons canola oil
1 cup Madeira	2 tablespoons plus 2 teaspoons aged
1 cup Chicken Stock (*see* recipe page 143)	balsamic vinegar (at least 12 years old)

To prepare the sauce:

Sauté 2 tablespoons of the bacon with the onions for 3 to 4 minutes, or until the onions are caramelized. Season the chicken livers with salt and pepper. Add the butter to the sauté pan and push the onions and bacon to the side of the pan. Add the chicken livers and cook for 3 to 4 minutes, or until golden brown. Add 3/4 cup of the Madeira and cook for 3 minutes, or until the wine is reduced by half. Puree the chicken liver mixture and the Chicken Stock until smooth and strain through a fine-mesh sieve. Cook the sauce for 5 minutes, or until warm. Season to taste with salt and pepper.

To prepare the collard greens:
Sauté the remaining 2 tablespoons of the bacon over medium-low heat for 2 minutes, or until most of the fat is rendered. Add the collard greens and cook for 3 minutes. Add the remaining 1/4 cup Madeira and cook for 4 minutes. Add the sugar and balsamic vinegar and cook for 2 to 3 minutes, or until the collard greens are tender. Season to taste with salt and pepper.

To prepare the scallops:
Season the scallops with salt and pepper. Place the canola oil in a hot sauté pan, add the scallops, and cook over medium heat for 2 minutes on each side, or until the scallops are lightly browned and just cooked.

Assembly:
Spread a circle of the chicken liver sauce on each plate. Place the collard greens on the sauce and top with 2 scallops. Drizzle the aged balsamic vinegar around the plates and top with freshly ground black pepper.

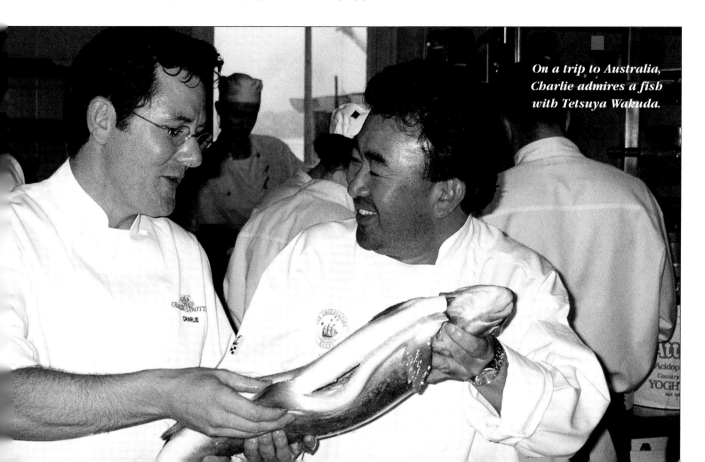

On a trip to Australia, Charlie admires a fish with Tetsuya Wakuda.

Grilled Beef Tenderloin Cobb Salad

Serves 4

1 shallot, minced

1/3 cup freshly squeezed lemon juice

2 tablespoons chopped fresh chives

1 cup olive oil

Salt and pepper

1 1/3 cups peeled and diced red
   and yellow tomatoes

8 cups mesclun salad mix

8 slices proscuitto, julienned

16 quail eggs, soft-boiled, peeled,
   and quartered

1 1/3 cups diced avocado

8 ounces beef tenderloin, grilled,
   cooled, and diced

1 1/3 cups crumbled blue cheese

12 grilled scallions, chilled and
   chopped

4 tablespoons chives (1-inch pieces)

To prepare the vinaigrette:

Place the shallot and lemon juice in a small bowl. Slowly whisk in the olive oil, fold in the chopped chives, and season to taste with salt and pepper.

To prepare the tomatoes:

Toss the diced tomatoes with 2 tablespoons of the vinaigrette and season to taste with salt and pepper.

To prepare the greens:

Toss the mesclun mix with half of the vinaigrette and season to taste with salt and pepper.

Assembly:

Arrange some of the mesclun greens to create a bed in the center of each plate. Arrange some of the proscuitto in a vertical line along the far left side of the greens. Starting next to the proscuitto, arrange the quail eggs, then the avocado, tomatoes, beef tenderloin, blue cheese, and scallions, each in individual lines to cover the mesclun mix completely. Top with freshly ground black pepper and sprinkle with the chive pieces. Drizzle the remaining vinaigrette over the salad.

Slow-Roasted Salmon with Red Wine Risotto, Wild Thyme, and Tiny White Asparagus

(From *Charlie Trotter's Seafood*)

Serves 4

1 clove garlic, minced

1/2 cup diced Spanish onions

2 tablespoons plus 1 teaspoon butter

1 cup uncooked Arborio rice

1 cup Red Wine Reduction
 (*see* recipe page 150)

1 cup roasted woodear mushrooms,
 chopped

Salt and pepper

4 3-ounce pieces salmon, skin removed

4 stalks celery, peeled and cut into long,
 thin strips

1 1 /2 cups fresh thyme

1 cup tiny white asparagus

1/2 cup Veal Stock Reduction
 (*see* recipe page 150)

To prepare the risotto:

Sweat the garlic and onion in a medium saucepan with 2 tablespoons of the butter. Add the Arborio rice, stir to coat with the onion and garlic, and cook for 3 minutes. Add 1/2 cup of the Red Wine Reduction and continue to cook over medium-low heat while stirring constantly but gently. Once the rice has absorbed the Red Wine Reduction, add the remaining 1/2 cup, stirring constantly. After all of the Red Wine Reduction is absorbed, add water in 1/4-cup increments until the rice is just cooked (it should be al dente yet creamy). Fold in the roasted woodear mushrooms and season to taste with salt and pepper.

To prepare the salmon:

Season both sides of the salmon with salt and pepper. Place the celery strips on a small sheet pan, creating a rack for the salmon. Place the salmon on top of the celery and cover with 1 1/4 cups fresh thyme. Roast at 225 F for 15 to 20 minutes, or until just done. Remove from oven, cut the celery into small dice, and fold into the red wine risotto.

To prepare the asparagus:

Quickly sauté the asparagus in a small pan with the remaining 1 teaspoon of butter. Season to taste with salt and pepper.

Assembly:

Place a small mound of the red wine risotto in the center of each plate and top with a piece of the salmon. Arrange some of the tiny white asparagus and remaining fresh thyme on top of the salmon. Warm the Veal Stock Reduction in a small saucepan and spoon it around the risotto.

Red Wine Reduction

Yield: 1/2 cup

1 Spanish onion, coarsely chopped	2 cloves garlic
1 carrot, coarsely cut	2 tablespoons grapeseed oil
1 stalk celery, coarsely chopped	1 750-Ml bottle Burgundy
1 Granny Smith apple, coarsely chopped	2 cups port
	1 cup Chicken Stock (*see* recipe below)

In a medium saucepan, caramelize the onion, carrots, celery, apples, and garlic in the grapeseed oil. Add the Burgundy and the port and simmer over medium heat for 2 hours. Strain and place in a small saucepan with the Chicken Stock. Continue to simmer over medium heat for 1 hour, or until reduced to 1/2 cup.

Chicken Stock for Red Wine Reduction

Yield: about 6 cups

10 pounds chicken bones	1 bulb garlic, cut in half
2 Spanish onions, coarsely chopped	1 bulb celery root, peeled and
2 carrots, coarsely chopped	chopped
4 stalks celery, coarsely chopped	1 tablespoon whole black peppercorns

Place all of the ingredients in a large stockpot. Cover with cold water (about 2 gallons). Bring to a boil, then reduce heat and simmer over medium heat for 4 hours, skimming away impurities that rise to the surface. Strain and reduce over medium heat for 45 minutes, or until reduced to about 6 cups.

Veal Stock Reduction

Yield: 1 1/4 cups

10 pounds veal bones	1 bulb garlic, cut in half
2 carrots, coarsely chopped	2 tablespoons grapeseed oil
2 stalks celery, coarsely chopped	1/2 cup tomato concassé
1 yellow onion, coarsely chopped	4 cups dry red wine (such as
1 leek, cleaned and coarsely chopped	Burgundy)

Place the bones in a roasting pan and roast in the oven at 450 F for 2 hours, or until golden brown. When bones are browned, caramelize the carrots, celery, onion, leek, and garlic in the grapeseed oil in a large stock pot. Add the tomato

concassé and cook for 5 minutes. Deglaze with the red wine and reduce until most of the wine has been cooked off. Add the browned bones and cover with cold water. Bring to a boil, then reduce heat and let simmer over medium heat for 8 hours. Strain through a fine-mesh sieve and simmer over medium heat for 45 minutes, or until it coats the back of a spoon. Extra reduction can be stored in the freezer for several months.

Apricot Basmati Rice Pudding with Apricot Juice and Lemongrass Anglaise

(From *Charlie Trotter's Vegetables*)

Serves 4

1/2 cup white basmati rice

1 cup milk

1/4 cup water

1/2 cup plus 3 tablespoons sugar

3 pieces of lemongrass (2 inches long)

2 cups apricot juice

8 small apricots, peeled

2 tablespoons chopped Hawaiian ginger

8 Brandy Snaps (*see* recipe page 152)

Lemongrass Anglaise (*see* recipe page 152)

To prepare the rice pudding:

Place the rice in a small saucepan with the milk, water, 1/3 cup of the sugar, and the lemongrass. Simmer over low heat for 20 to 30 minutes. You may need to add some water if the milk is absorbed before the rice is cooked. Remove and discard the lemongrass, and set aside at room temperature.

To prepare the apricot reduction and the apricots:

Place the apricot juice in a small saucepan and reduce over medium heat for 30 minutes, or until reduced to 1/3 cup. Strain through a fine-mesh sieve and set aside. Cut 4 apricots into small dice and sauté over medium heat for 3 minutes with 2 tablespoons of the sugar and the Hawaiian ginger. Cut the remaining 4 apricots into thin slices.

Assembly:

Place one Brandy Snap in the center of each plate. Place a small ring mold on top of the Brandy Snap and fill with a layer of rice. Top with some of the diced apricot and place another Brandy Snap on top of the apricot. Spread another layer of rice over the Brandy Snap and arrange the sliced apricots in a pinwheel on top of the rice. Sprinkle the apricots with 1 tablespoon of sugar and lightly caramelize the sugar with a blowtorch. Remove the mold. Spoon the Lemongrass Anglaise and the apricot reduction around the plate.

Brandy Snaps
Yield: 8 snaps

2 tablespoons butter, softened

1/4 cup confectioners' sugar

2 tablespoons honey

2 tablespoons brandy

1/3 cup flour

Pinch of salt

Place the butter and sugar in a small bowl. Combine with a fork, add the honey and brandy, and stir until smooth. Add the flour and salt, and stir until smooth. Place 8 rounded teaspoons of batter on a nonstick sheet pan about 2 inches apart, and spread into 1-1/2-inch circles. Place in the oven at 350 F for 3 to 5 minutes, or until golden brown. Once slightly cool, remove from the pan.

Lemongrass Anglaise
Yield: 1 cup

2 egg yolks

4 teaspoons sugar

1 cup heavy cream

1/4 cup chopped lemongrass

In a bowl, whisk together the yolks and sugar until smooth. Place the heavy cream and lemongrass in a small saucepan and bring to a boil over medium heat. Pour the hot cream into the bowl and, whipping constantly, allow the cream to temper the yolks. Return the mixture to the saucepan and cook over medium heat, stirring constantly for 2 minutes, or until it coats the back of a spoon. Do not boil the mixture. Strain through a fine-mesh sieve and cool.

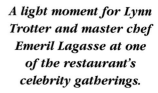

A light moment for Lynn Trotter and master chef Emeril Lagasse at one of the restaurant's celebrity gatherings.

Whole Roasted Figs with Goat Cheese Ice Cream, Spicy Fig Sauce, and Oatmeal Tuiles
Serves 6

2 tablespoons unsalted butter

1/4 cup confectioners' sugar

1 1/2 teaspoons finely chopped lemon zest

3 tablespoons honey

1/3 cup flour

3 tablespoons rolled oats, lightly toasted

12 fresh figs

1/2 cup Simple Syrup (*see* note page 142)

2 tablespoons port

6 tablespoons heavy cream

2 ounces goat cheese

2 tablespoons granulated sugar

Goat Cheese Ice Cream (*see* recipe page 154)

Spicy Fig Sauce (*see* recipe page 154)

1 tablespoon baby thyme sprigs

To make the tuiles:

Cream the butter, confectioners' sugar, and lemon zest. Add the honey and the flour and mix well. Spread about 1/2 teaspoon of the batter onto a Silpat-lined or nonstick sheet pan. Use a small offset spatula to spread the tuile into a 1-3/4-inch circle. Repeat the process, making at least 18 tuiles (the extras will allow for breakage). Sprinkle the top of each tuile with a pinch of rolled oats, reserving 1/2 tablespoon for garnish. Bake at 350 F for 5 minutes, or until golden brown. (The tuiles may be cut with a ring cutter after cooking, for a more precise shape.) Immediately transfer the tuiles to a countertop or other flat surface to cool.

To prepare the figs:

Cut off the tops of 6 of the figs. Use a small spoon to press a cavity into each fig and dip the whole fig in the Simple Syrup. Fill the figs with the port. (If there are holes in the bottoms of the figs, cut small pieces off the tops to fill the holes.) Place the filled figs on a sheet pan and bake at 350 F for 25 minutes, or until they have softened. Slice the remaining 6 figs in half lengthwise to create 1/4-inch-thick slices. Warm the slices in the remaining Simple Syrup.

To prepare the goat cheese cream:

Thoroughly combine 2 tablespoons of the heavy cream with the goat cheese and granulated sugar. Whisk the remaining 1/4 cup cream until it reaches soft peaks and fold it into the goat cheese mixture.

Assembly:

Place 3 to 4 fig slices on one side of each plate. Place a small spoonful of the goat cheese cream on the figs and top with a tuile. Put a small spoonful of the cream on top of the stack and add 3 to 4 fig slices, another spoonful of cream, and a tuile. Build another layer with a spoonful of cream, figs, another spoonful of cream, and a tuile. Place a roasted fig alongside the stacked figs and top with a quenelle of Goat Cheese Ice Cream. Spoon the Spicy Fig Sauce around the plates and sprinkle with thyme sprigs and the remaining 1/2 tablespoon of rolled oats.

■

Charlie Palmer of Aureole, New York City; Norman Van Aken; and Daniel Boulud join Trotter to whip up a meal at the James Beard House in Manhattan.

Goat Cheese Ice Cream
Yield: approximately 3 cups

2 cups heavy cream	1/4 cup sugar
1/2 cup milk	3 tablespoons corn syrup
4 egg yolks	4 ounces goat cheese

Prepare an ice-water bath. Bring the cream and milk to a boil. Whisk together the egg yolks and sugar, and slowly pour in some of the hot cream to temper the eggs. Pour the eggs into the cream and continue to cook for 2 to 3 minutes, or until the mixture coats the back of a spoon and steam rises to the top. Whisk together the corn syrup and the goat cheese, and then whisk this mixture into the cream mixture until smooth. Strain through a fine-mesh sieve and chill over the ice-water bath. Freeze in an ice-cream machine. Keep frozen until ready to use.

Spicy Fig Sauce
Yield: 1/2 cup

2 tablespoons sugar	1/2 cup chopped fresh figs
1/4 cup freshly squeezed	1 star anise
orange juice, warm	3 whole black peppercorns

Cook the sugar in a heavy-bottomed sauté pan over medium heat for 3 minutes, or until golden brown. Add the orange juice and bring to a boil. Add the figs, star anise, and peppercorns, bring to a boil and cook for 3 minutes. Remove from the heat and strain through a fine-mesh sieve, pushing on the solids to remove as much liquid as possible. If necessary, thin with a little warm water to a sauce consistency.

INDEX

Photograph © Tim Turner